The Nine Faces of Fear

POSTMODERN ETHICS SERIES

Postmodernism and deconstruction are usually associated with a destruction of ethical values. The volumes in the Postmodern Ethics series demonstrate that such views are mistaken because they ignore the religious element that is at the heart of existential-postmodern philosophy. This series aims to provide a space for thinking about questions of ethics in our times. When many voices are speaking together from unlimited perspectives within the postmodern labyrinth, what sort of ethics can there be for those who believe there is a way through the dark night of technology and nihilism beyond exclusively humanistic offerings? The series invites any careful exploration of the postmodern and the ethical.

Series Editors:

Marko Zlomislic (Conestoga College)
† David Goicoechea (Brock University)

Other Volumes in the Series:

Cross and Khôra: Deconstruction and Christianity in the Work of John D. Caputo edited by Neal DeRoo and Marko Zlomislić

Agape and Personhood with Kierkegaard, Mother, and Paul (A Logic of Reconciliation from the Shamans to Today) by David Goicoechea

The Poverty of Radical Orthodoxy edited by Lisa Isherwood and Marko Zlomislić

Theologies of Liberation in Palestine-Israel: Indigenous, Contextual, and Postcolonial Perspectives edited by Nur Masalha and Lisa Isherwood

Agape and the Four Loves with Nietzsche, Father, and Q (A Physiology of Reconciliation from the Greeks to Today) by David Goicoechea

Fundamentalism and Gender: Scripture—Body—Community edited by Ulrike Auga, Christina von Braun, Claudia Bruns, and Jana Husmann

The Nine Faces of Fear

Ego, Enneatype, Essence

STEPHEN J. COSTELLO

POSTMODERN ETHICS SERIES 11

PICKWICK *Publications* · Eugene, Oregon

THE NINE FACES OF FEAR
Ego, Enneatype, Essence

Postmodern Ethics Series 11

Copyright © 2022 Stephen J. Costello. All rights reserved. Except for brief quotations in critical publications or reviews, no part of this book may be reproduced in any manner without prior written permission from the publisher. Write: Permissions, Wipf and Stock Publishers, 199 W. 8th Ave., Suite 3, Eugene, OR 97401.

Pickwick Publications
An Imprint of Wipf and Stock Publishers
199 W. 8th Ave., Suite 3
Eugene, OR 97401

www.wipfandstock.com

PAPERBACK ISBN: 978-1-6667-3014-2
HARDCOVER ISBN: 978-1-6667-2126-3
EBOOK ISBN: 978-1-6667-2127-0

Cataloguing-in-Publication data:

> Names: Costello, Stephen J., author.
>
> Title: The nine faces of fear : ego, enneatype, essence / by Stephen J. Costello.
>
> Description: Eugene, OR: Pickwick Publications, 2022 | Postmodern Ethics Series | Includes bibliographical references.
>
> Identifiers: ISBN 978-1-6667-3014-2 (paperback) | ISBN 978-1-6667-2126-3 (hardcover) | ISBN 978-1-6667-2127-0 (ebook)
>
> Subjects: LCSH: Fear. | Enneagram. | Ethics. | Logotherapy.

Classification: RC489.L6 C67 2022 (print) | RC489.L6 (ebook)

Scriptures marked (TLV) are taken from the Tree of Life®, TLV®. Copyright © 2016 by Messianic Jewish Family Bible Society. Used by permission of Baker Books.

Scripture quotations marked (NIV) are taken from the Holy Bible, New International Version®, NIV®. Copyright © 1973, 1978, 1984, 2011 by Biblica, Inc.™ Used by permission of Zondervan.

Scriptures marked (NJB) are taken from From The Jerusalem Bible © 1966 by Darton Longman & Todd Ltd and Doubleday and Company Ltd.

Scriptures marked (KJV) are taken from the King James Version, public domain.

01/05/22

I dedicate this book to my parents, Val and Johnny,
in loving gratitude.

If you know the enemy and know yourself, you need not fear the results of a hundred battles.

—Sun Tzu

Love is not an emotion, it's your very existence.

—Rumi

All emotions are pure which gather you and lift you up; that emotion is impure which seizes only one side of your being and so distorts you.

—Rilke

Spacious mind does not negate narrow mind but embraces and includes it in a larger vision. In this way your sense of self is freed from fear and anger, and you are empowered to engage the world with your own unique expression of lovingkindness.

—Rabbi Rami Shapiro

Fear thou not, for I am with thee.

—*Isaiah (41:10 KJV)*

The quiet words of the wise are more to be heeded than the shouting of a ruler among fools.

—*Ecclesiastes (9:17 NIV)*

Do not let your hearts be troubled or afraid.

—*John (14:27 NJB)*

Contents

Preface | ix
Acknowledgements | xiii
Introduction: Feelings vs Facts | xv

1 What Is Fear? The Alchemy of an Emotion | 1
2 Formulations on Fear | 28
3 Fear in Stoic Theory and Therapy | 49
4 The Enneagram: Nine Foundational Fears | 63
   Conclusion | 113

Postscript: From Fear to Freedom | 117
Bibliography | 121

Preface

"If we can winter this one out, we can summer anywhere."
—Seamus Heaney

WE ARE WITNESSING A trio of contemporary crises: credit, Covid, and climate. COVID-19 provided the tragic, unpredictable context for the completion of this book during the latter half of 2020 and the first quarter of 2021. The Coronavirus pandemic created a culture of fear and panic which swept the country and the world, affecting us all in unimaginable ways, from self-isolation and cocooning through social distancing and lockdown to death. We all had to draw deep on our inner resources and strength of spirit in the face of such a crisis. Three things are needed for resilience in a time of terror: a sense of control, purpose, and hope. Daily life changed inexorably overnight. Negative news was an hourly feature, leaving us all uncertain, upset, and forlorn. World statistics formed the basis of many online conversations. Behavioral economists told us that 15 percent of the population would behave appallingly selfishly. But there were other figures. Here in Ireland, within a few days of the global virus breaking out, fifty thousand people had volunteered for work in hospitals—demonstrating heroic virtue.

We were deprived of family, friends, and finances, cut off from human contact. Every smile from a stranger, as we sought to keep our six-feet distance on the footpath, seared into our souls. It was a tacit communication that we were all in this together. Never before did our planet seem so fragile

Preface

and inter-connected, our lives so precarious and vulnerable. It's said that even a faint flutter of a butterfly's wings can have cosmic consequences. We saw that unhygienic conditions in a Chinese food market in Wuhan could bring all humanity to its knees. Life, as we knew it, was profoundly altered and we wondered whether there an end in sight, a light at the end of the tunnel, and what might "the new normal" look like.

I have noticed in the last year four types of Coronavirus character: the bored, the brazen, the blissful, and the broken. The bored are frustrated and fed up, lethargic and languishing in the existential vacuum. The brazen are the libertarian 'Covidiots' who resent any restrictions on their personal liberty (the anti-mask, anti-vaccine brigade). The blissful live in a bubble and to a large extent remain unaffected by the pandemic either through intentional ignorance, financial independence, or enlightenment. The broken are those suffering from mental health issues, distressed and depressed, and sometimes suicidal. There has been an inordinate hyperreflection on Covid which has produced a toxic negativity, so much so that it seems we're all experiencing OCD—Obsessive Covid Disorder. Dereflection is the movement of the attention out toward what is positive and joyful, to what pulls rather than pushes us, to what draws rather than what drives us or, worse, drags us down.

In ancient Greek times, the plague came after bad leadership. Socrates experienced the Plague of Athens (430 BC, which lasted four years and killed over one-third of the population); legend had it that due to his discipline he was one of the few men who escaped infection. Marcus Aurelius, the Stoic Emperor, wrote his famous *Meditations* in the middle of one of the worst plagues in European history. The Antonine Plague, named after him, was estimated to have killed up to five million people, possibly including Marcus himself. Stoics, like Marcus Aurelius, would suggest that fear does us more harm than the things of which we're afraid.

What we need now is great governance and wise leadership at the political level, solidarity and compassion at the social level, and reason in the mind and love in the heart at the individual level. We don't know what magnificent moment still awaits us. After the three-year long Bubonic Plague (1347–50)—or "Black Death"—in Mediaeval Europe, which killed as many as one-third of Europe's people (an estimated thirty million), came the Italian Renaissance.

Preface

Plague of an Ancient City by Michiel Sweerts (c. 1652–54).

The sun shines above, over the sometimes sad human scene, reminding us that the Self is always present—the spirit always at work in the world. We can spend our time actualizing creative, experiential and, above all, attitudinal values, especially in the face of unbearable suffering and blows of fate. Charles Dickens's opening words from *A Tale of Two Cities* seem so apposite, sound the right note: "It was the best of times, it was the worst of times, it was the age of wisdom, it was the age of foolishness, it was the epoch of belief, it was the epoch of incredulity, it was the season of light, it was the season of darkness, it was the spring of hope, it was the winter of despair."

When things were at their worst, we will want to say that we were at our best. In *The Plague*, Albert Camus made the point that true exile was in one's own home. We surrendered our liberty out of love. A Platonic triad suggests itself:

1: Search for meaning. Man is a being in search of meaning.

2: Love a little more. Plato: "Love is the joy of the Good, the wonder of the wise, and the amazement of the gods."[1]

---

1. Plato, *Symposium*, 197d.

Preface

3: Pause; fall still; meditate. Plato: "When the soul contemplates in herself, by herself, she passes into the realm of the pure, the eternal, the undying and unchanging. She ceases wandering and she is unmoving."[2]

These lines of J. R. R. Tolkien, from *The Lord of the Rings: The Fellowship of the Ring*, surely resonate with us all: "I wish it need not have happened in my time", said Frodo. "So do I", said Gandalf, "and so do all who live to see such times. But that is not for them to decide. All we have to decide is what to do with the time that is given us." Viktor Frankl, for his part, once remarked that we are not responsible for the time in which we live, but we are responsible for the extent to which we help to shape or counter these currents.

T. S. Eliot famously described April as the cruelest month, and it is tempting to see all months as such during a lengthy global health emergency. However, let the quotation below serve as a more fitting epigraph for this book.

"Plunge into the deep without fear, with the gladness of April in your heart." –Tagore

---

2. Plato, *Phaedo*, 79d.

Acknowledgements

MY HEARTFELT THANKS TO my family, especially my parents, Val and Johnny, together with my friends, in particular Darren Cleary, Derek Smyth, Tom O'Connor, and Brendan Kavanagh of Olive Media who saw the potential in my work, for all your encouragement, sustained interest, and enthusiastic support. My gratitude also goes to Michael Ryan (a fellow seven on the Enneagram!) of the School of Philosophy who gave a memorable seminar on the Enneagram to my logotherapy students, and from whom I have learnt so much.

Introduction: Feelings vs Facts

It is said that before entering the sea
a river trembles with fear.

She looks back at the path she has travelled,
from the peaks of the mountains,
the long winding road crossing forests and villages.

And in front of her,
she sees an ocean so vast,
that to enter
there seems nothing more than to disappear forever.

But there is no other way.
The river can not go back.

Nobody can go back.
To go back is impossible in existence.

The river needs to take the risk
of entering the ocean
because only then will fear disappear,
because that's where the river will know
it's not about disappearing into the ocean,
but of becoming the ocean.

"Fear," by Khalil Gibran

Introduction: Feelings vs Facts

What Is Fear?

"Ignorance is the cause of fear." –Seneca

Is fear a feeling? In *Philosophical Investigations*, Ludwig Wittgenstein asks a number of pertinent questions: What is fear? What does "being afraid" mean? If I wanted to explain it at a single showing, I would *act* fear, he says. "I'm afraid" is not always a description of a state of mind. Wittgenstein wonders what does "I'm afraid" really mean; what do I aim at when I say it? And, of course, no answer is forthcoming, or only an inadequate one. The question is: "In what sort of context does it occur?" What cannot be said, must be shown. Describing my state of mind is something we do in context. The *use* teaches us the meaning. So, "I'm afraid" and "I'm afraid I can't come to your party tomorrow," differ radically. Wittgenstein makes a distinction between the *object* of fear and the *cause* of fear. A face which inspires fear or delight (the object of fear or delight) is not on that account its cause, but—one might say—its target. For example, the object of fear may be a spider, but that is not the cause, which has nothing to do with the spider at all, as a perceptual object but rather everything to do with a conception we have of the spider, a story we've put onto the spider (projection).

Freedom from Fear

"It is fear that I am most afraid of." –Michel de Montaigne

The freedom from fear is a fundamental human right, according to the *Universal Declaration of Human Rights*. Franklin D. Roosevelt called it one of the "Four Freedoms" (January 6, 1941) in his famous State of the Union speech—the historical context of which was the reduction of armaments. The Four Fundamental Freedoms, which everyone everywhere ought to enjoy, are:

1. Freedom of Speech
2. Freedom of Worship
3. Freedom from Want
4. Freedom from Fear

Introduction: Feelings vs Facts

Painting by Guido Reni c. 1611.

This influenced the American painter Norman Rockwell in 1943 to create *Freedom from Fear*—in his series of four paintings called *Four Freedoms*. His *Freedom from Fear* features last and is reproduced below.

Introduction: Feelings vs Facts

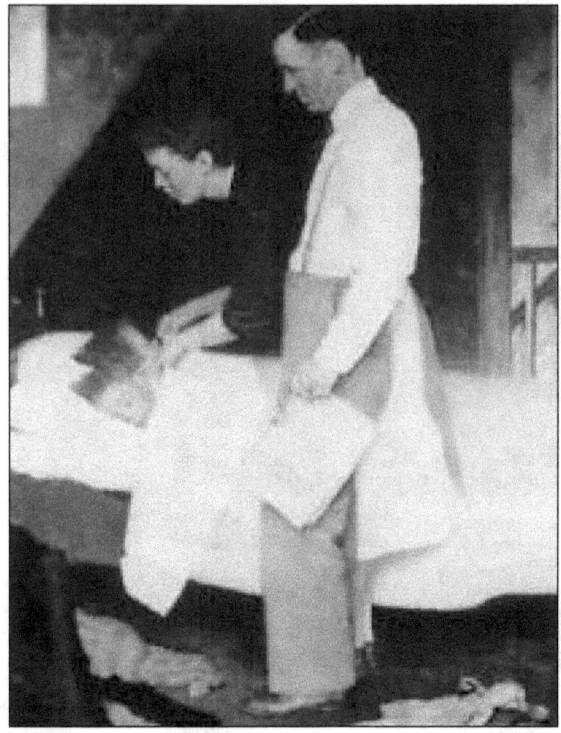

The Formation of Feelings

If the principal aim of human life is inner freedom, and if fear is one of the major impediments to freedom, we need to see how this feeling of fear is formed.

Your thoughts produce your feelings. If a brain scan was hooked up to you one could see what it looks like when you have a thought—a pulse of electrical activity occurs which stimulates the release of chemicals called neuropeptides that will communicate with your body to produce a feeling. *The thoughts you have determine how you feel.*

Feelings combine, coalesce. For example, fear and anger are inextricably interlinked. Anger is a fear-based form of self-defense. Anger is a reaction to fear, to a perceived threat. Emotions, which are always multi-layered, cause other emotions. If you feel confused or worried, you may also feel anxious. Disappointment may be accompanied by sadness, just as disgust can cause shame, and shame can provoke embarrassment. Physiologically, fear and anger are very similar, with virtually the same effects on the autonomic nervous system with respect to respiratory, cardiovascular and electrodermal means (neural interactions). Emotions are like chain-reactions; they are interconnected, conjoined. Anger can mask fear. When fear arises, anger is not far behind. First fear, then anger, as twin tyrants of the mercurial mind.

Yoda, the Grand Master of the Jedi in *Star Wars*, who is an archetype of the senex (sage), being over eight hundred years old, symbolizes the two-million-year-old Self in all of us, sums up the wisdom of the ages when he famously says: "Fear is the path to the dark side. Fear leads to anger. Anger leads to hate. Hate leads to suffering." We can distinguish *four* kinds of feelings:

1. Pleasant feelings
2. Unpleasant feelings
3. Neutral feelings
4. Mixed feelings

Feelings follow this universal fourfold path:

1. They are born
2. They manifest
3. They stay for a while
4. They pass on

We can observe our feelings as if from a riverbank rather than becoming embroiled, entangled and enmeshed in them. We can notice what passes and what remains. We needn't identify with our feelings because we are more than our feelings, just as we are more than our thoughts.

Psychologists have identified *six* basic emotions: happiness, sadness, disgust, fear, surprise, and anger. Other ones include pride, shame, embarrassment, and excitement. Emotions form a wheel, much like colors.

> "If you look into your own heart, and you find nothing wrong there, what is there to worry about? What is there to fear?" –Confucius

> "Of all base passions, fear is most accursed."[3]

---

3. William Shakespeare, *Henry VI, Part 1*, 5.2.18.

Introduction: Feelings vs Facts

Toxins, trauma, and thoughts can wreak havoc on the body, mind, and heart, leading to calamitous results. But we are not born with fear or anger. Fear and anger are brought about by our experiences as much as by our expectations, by what we've seen or read, by what other people have told us—their stories. The mind can be both foe and friend, depending on how we use it. "As a man thinketh, so he shall be."

There are so many schools of thought about the emotions, ranging from Buddhism to existentialism, to name but two. There is no universally accepted taxonomy or theory of the emotions. What is put forward here is a philosophy that I would ask you to consider without accepting or rejecting. Test it against your own personal experience. It is intended as a practical guide. I will draw from the great philosophical traditions of both East (Advaita Vedanta) and West (Plato and the Stoics), as well as on the Enneagram system, which is the bridge between them. Just as the brain has two hemispheres which need integrating, so too must we synthesize the perennial wisdom of both Orient and Occident. I write as a philosopher and logoanalyst, but I am interested too in what works. So, I present here a practical philosophical and psycho-therapeutic programme of sorts. The aim in a nutshell: to help you transcend your fear.

"Conquer anger by non-anger." –Buddha

"There is no fear for one whose mind is not filled with desires."
–Buddha

Seven Ingredients of EQ

Experts on emotional intelligence highlight *seven* important ingredients—which I call the "7 Cs" so necessary for self-regulation and equilibrium:

1. *Confidence*: mastery over body and behavior
2. *Curiosity*: positive, pleasurable interest
3. *Contribution*: having a meaningful influence/impact
4. *Control* of the ego: ability to manage and monitor moods
5. *Connectivity*: relating to and engaging with others
6. *Capacity* to communicate: the authentic exchange of feelings and ideas

7. *Cooperation*: balancing one's own needs with others'

> "Anger is an acid that can do more harm to the vessel in which it is stored than to anything on which it is poured." –Mark Twain

Confidence, creativity, curiosity, connectivity, contribution, and true communication/conversation stem not from the ever-active ego but from the still Self, when we dis-identify from our feelings especially those of fear.

Seven Suggestions

But for now, even before we begin, let me enumerate *seven* suggestions which will become elaborated on as we proceed:

- Try to stay in the present moment.
- Observe your emotions—your fear and anger—but do not partake in either.
- Become attentive to the kindness of others.
- Act with compassion and understanding. Go gently.
- Use wisdom to analyze your feelings.
- Approach problems with patience and reason.
- Practice the substitution method: replace the negative with a positive, focusing on what is joyful.

Facts and Feelings

Feelings come and go. But *feelings are not facts*, by which I mean, they are not necessarily in accord with reality—with that which is (outside your mind). They are *subjective*, not *objective*. They tell a *story* not the *truth*.

Imagine, if you will, that one side of your brain deals in facts and the other side deals in stories or interpretations about these facts. When you find yourself in a loop of exaggerated stories about what is going

Introduction: Feelings vs Facts

on—stories you have told yourself, fed yourself, ask: 'What are the facts here?' Become like a scientist or sage. Question yourself. Become more aware, more detached, less identified with all your moods which toss you around hither and thither like a doll, so you behave like a teenager or two-year-old throwing a tantrum. It is no way to live. If fear and anger (to name just two emotions) are blocks or barriers—injurious impediments to happiness, then the Self, as distinct from our ego, operates in the system by being more of a beta-blocker, for, in its pure state, or better, *as* a pure state, it knows only bliss.

> "Everything we hear is an opinion, not a fact. Everything we see is a perspective, not the truth." –Marcus Aurelius

This study is a sketch; it does not presume to be an exhaustive exegesis. It's intended for the general reader. Needless to say, the short accounts here of Vedic philosophy, Stoicism, and the Enneagram system all warrant separate treatments consisting of full-length books devoted to each topic. However, one advantage of keeping things tight is that there is a thread of continuity across the *three* doctrines I discuss, which will become apparent. It is a companion volume to my *Beyond Hope: Philosophical Reflections*.

I present a number of principles and propositions. It is for the reader to adopt these for themselves in overcoming fears and facing into them, so that they are no longer felt as overwhelming. The aim is to present a toolkit of both philosophical wisdom and practical insight. There are stories, parables, existential exercises, 'questions for consideration', and 'the practice', on which to pause and ponder, so that the teaching becomes embodied, engaged with, and implemented. I include a number of quotations/sayings per page, which are intended as koans to provoke Self-reflection as well as anchors to ground the reader.

My method, if that's what it is, is to swirl around the subject matter from different angles, by way of a *rotazione*, a *circumambulatio* that weaves the strands together in order to reinforce, strengthen, and support my philosophizing on the fascinating subject of fear.

The answer to both fear (and anger) is ultimately to awaken to the deepest dimension of oneself—One Self. As such, it's a journey into the heart of being.

> "Caminante, no hay camino, se hace camino al andar."
> –Antonio Machado

Introduction: Feelings vs Facts

("Journeyman, there is no path; you make your own path as you walk"; my translation)

We are afraid of things which need not be feared, and we desire things which are not necessary. There is perhaps no better a description of what I am up to in this book than the beautiful one given by Plato in the last work written by him—the *Laws*, in which he writes in Book X: "What you do not see, in your little corner of the mighty universe, is that things do not happen in it for your sake: you, like all that takes place there, are what you are in order that its perfection may be complete."[4]

* * *

Quotations and citations are taken from the following—listed in alphabetical order:

Aristotle (384–322 BC): Greek philosopher, founder of the Lyceum

Assagioli, Roberto (1888–1974): Italian psychiatrist and founder of psychosynthesis

Aurelius, Marcus (AD 121–180): Roman emperor and Stoic philosopher

Bacon, Francis (1561–1626): English philosopher, father of empiricism

Beck, Aaron (1921–present): American psychiatrist and father of cognitive behavioral therapy (CBT)

Buddha, Gautama (563/480–483/400 BC): Indian philosopher, founder of Buddhism

Campbell, Joseph (1904–1987): American mythologist

Char, René (1907–1988): French poet

Confucius (551–479 BC): Chinese philosopher, founder of Confucianism

Curie, Marie (1867–1934): French-Polish physicist and chemist

---

4. Plato, *Laws*, 903b.

Introduction: Feelings vs Facts

Descartes, René (1596–1650): French philosopher and mathematician

Eckhart, Meister, OP (1260–1328): German Dominican philosopher and mystic

Ellis, Albert (1913–2007): American psychologist and founder of Rational Emotive Behavior Therapy

Emerson, Ralph Waldo (1803–1882): American philosopher

Epictetus (55–135 AD): Greek slave and Stoic philosopher

Epicurus (341–270 BC): Ancient Greek philosopher, founder of Epicureanism.

Frankl, Viktor (1905–1997): Austrian neurologist, psychiatrist, philosopher, and founder of logotherapy and existential analysis

Gandhi, Mahatma (1869–1948): Leader of Indian independence

Gibran, Kahlil (1883–1931): Lebanese poet

Goethe, Johann Wolfgang von (1749–1832): German writer and statesman

Gurdjieff, George Ivanovich (1866–1949): Russian philosopher and spiritual teacher; called his school 'the Fourth Way'

Hanh, Thich Nhat (1926–present): Vietnamese monk, Zen Buddhist

Heaney, Seamus (1939–2013): Irish poet and playwright; Nobel Laureate in Literature

Hillesum, Etty (1914–1943): Dutch author of spiritual diaries; killed in Auschwitz

Hoover, Herbert (1874–1964): 31st President of the United States

Ignatius of Loyola, St. (1491–1556): Basque priest and founder of the Jesuit Order

James, William (1842–1910): American philosopher and psychologist

Jung, C. G. (1875–1961): Swiss psychiatrist

Kavanagh, Patrick (1904–1967): Irish poet

Keller, Helen (1880–1968): Deaf-blind American author

Introduction: Feelings vs Facts

Kipling, Rudyard (1865–1936): Indian-born English poet

Lonergan, Bernard, SJ (1904–1984): Canadian Jesuit philosopher and theologian

Machado, Antonio (1875–1939): Spanish poet and leading member of the Generation of '98.

Mandela, Nelson (1918–2013): South African anti-apartheid political leader and one-time president

Milton, John (1608–1678): English poet

Montaigne, Michel de (1533–1592): Philosopher of the French Renaissance

Murdoch, Iris (1919–1999): Irish-British philosopher and novelist

Ouspensky, Pyotr (1878–1947): Russian esotericist and expositor of Gurdjieff's doctrines

Plato (c. 429–347 BC): Athenian philosopher, founder of the Academy

Plotinus (AD 204–270): Greek philosopher, author of the *Enneads*

Plutchik, Robert (1927–2006): American psychologist

Roosevelt, Franklin D. (1882–1945): 32nd US president

Rilke, Rainer Maria (1875–1926): Austrian mystic poet and novelist

Rufus, Musonius Gaius (AD 25–95): Roman Stoic philosopher

Rumi (1207–1273): Persian poet and Sufi mystic

Russell, Bertrand (1872–1970): British philosopher and Nobel laureate

Saraswati, Shantanand (1913–1993): Shankaracharya of the Jyotir Math monastery

Seneca, the Younger (c. 4 BC–65 AD): Roman Stoic philosopher and statesman

Shakespeare, William (1564–1616): English poet and playwright and the world's greatest dramatist

Introduction: Feelings vs Facts

Sivananda, Sri Swami (1887–1963): Hindu spiritual teacher; founder of the Divine Life Society

Socrates (c. 470–399 BC): One of the founders of Western philosophy

Sophocles (497/6–406/5): Greek tragedian

Spinoza, Baruch (1632–1677): Dutch Enlightenment, rationalist philosopher

Tagore, Rabindranath (1861–1941): Indian poet and polymath

Tzu, Lao (unknown; 6th–4th century BC): Chinese philosopher and founder of Taoism

Tzu, Sun (544–496 BC): Chinese General and philosopher

Twain, Mark (1835–1910): American writer

Upanishads: part of the Vedas—ancient Sanskrit texts of Hinduism

Vivekananda, Swami (1863–1902): Indian Hindu monk and disciple of Ramakrishna

Wilde, Oscar (1854–1900): Irish playwright and poet

Wittgenstein, Ludwig (1889–1951): Austrian-British philosopher

* * *

Authors consulted on the Enneagram system include the following, all of which I warmly recommend: Tad Dunne's *Enneatypes* (whom in a private communication with the author suggested that the Enneagram is a proto-analysis, serving as a generalization about a person's predominant concerns), Sandra Maitri's *The Spiritual Dimension of the Enneagram*; Richard Rohr's *Discovering the Enneagram*; Jerome Wagner's *Nine Lenses on the World: The Enneagram Perspective*; and Riso and Hudson's *The Wisdom of the Enneagram*. Indeed, my outline of the Enneagram is, in large measure, a *précis* of the above, especially Riso and Rohr.

This work, ostensibly different from two others I have written in this series—*Dynamics of Discernment* and *Between Speech and Silence*—comprises, due to a certain thematic consonance, a trilogy of kinds.

1

What Is Fear? The Alchemy of an Emotion

Introduction

"To conquer fear is the beginning of wisdom." –Bertrand Russell

ROBERT PLUTCHIK, A TWENTIETH-CENTURY American psychologist, made a special study of the emotions. He proposed a psycho-evolutionary classification of emotional responses. His "wheel of the emotions," reproduced below, depicts what he considered to be the *eight* primary emotions:[1]

1. Joy
2. Trust
3. Fear
4. Surprise
5. Sadness
6. Anticipation
7. Anger
8. Disgust

He also identified several primary, secondary and tertiary dyads. Furthermore, each primary emotion has a polar opposite so that:

1. Plutchik, *The Emotions*.

The Nine Faces of Fear

1. Joy is the opposite of sadness
2. Fear is the opposite of anger
3. Anticipation is the opposite of surprise
4. Disgust is the opposite of trust

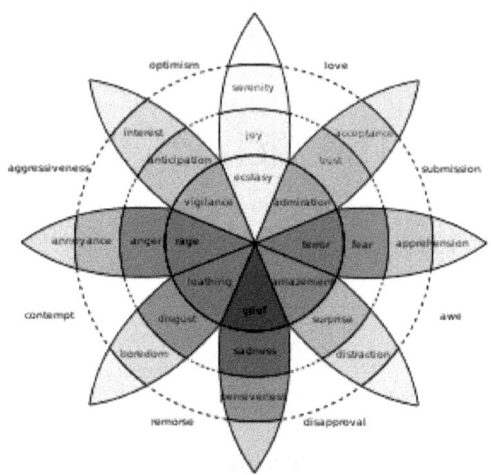

For Plutchik, fear is a basic emotion, and its opposite is anger not courage. The courageous individual experiences fear so courage is not fear's opposite—fear just doesn't dominate the courageous person. He or she feels fear but faces through it and goes beyond it.

"Courage is knowing what not to fear." –Plato

Plato discusses courage in the *Laches*, which he defines as knowing what not to fear. The discussion involves Socrates and two Generals—Laches and Nicias—who were both active in the Peloponnesian war. (Nicias was captured and put to death). At the outset, courage is defined as wisdom about what is to be feared. Laches maintains that courage is remaining at one's post and defending oneself against one's enemy without running away. But this is an *example* not the *essence* of courage, which Socrates defines as the "wise endurance of the soul."[2] Fear is interpreted by Plato in the *Laws* as the expectation of a future evil or the expectation to pain just as confidence

2. Plato, *Laches*, 192b.

is the expectation to pleasure. Ones that inspire hope, by contrast, are either future non-evils or future goods. As seventeenth-century Dutch philosopher Baruch Spinoza put it: "Anything whatever can be the accidental cause of hope or fear."

> "The fear of death is indeed the pretense of wisdom, and not real wisdom, being the appearance of knowing the unknown."
> –Plato

> "There is no hope unmingled with fear, and no fear unmingled with hope." –Spinoza

For Plato, there are *two* kinds of fear: (1) common fear which is this expectation of evil (pain); and (2) the fear of other peoples' bad opinion of us, which is shame. In his ethics, Aristotle, Plato's student, had placed courage as the midpoint between boldness and fear. So, boldness in times of fear is courage (fortitude).

> "He who has overcome his fears becomes truly free." –Aristotle

The Roman Stoic philosopher, Seneca the Younger, for his part, gave advice to his nephew Lucillius on fear, devoting his thirteenth letter, "On Groundless Fears," to the subject, where he penned the famous phrase: "There are more things, Lucillius, likely to frighten us than there are to crush us; we suffer more in imagination than in reality."[3] So, fear and courage are played out in the mind. Things torment us more than they ought. We are in the habit of exaggerating, imagining, or anticipating sorrow. This is the result of being held captive by our swirling thoughts—those mosquitoes of the mind. "We do not put to the test those things which cause our fear."[4] We need to examine the essence of fear, so. Essence is that by which a thing is what it is. The truth of being is essence. The mind fashions for itself false shapes when there are no signs of them. It twists things in thought.

> "There is nothing so certain among those objects of fear that it is not more certain still that things we dread sink into nothing and that things we hope for mock us." –Seneca

---

3. Seneca, *Moral Essays*, 13.4.
4. Seneca, *Moral Essays*, 13.4.

The Nine Faces of Fear

We need to weigh our fears, see them in the true light of consciousness. If fear is winning out, incline towards hope. The worst-case scenario may not happen and where will all your worrying get you? Jesus was reported by to have asked which of us by worrying can add a single hour to his span of life. Be not anxious. Most fears are unfounded. The mind has a strange tendency, Seneca observes, to seem to function independently of external events. He describes the exhausting habit we have of creating imaginary disasters in the mind.

So, what is fear? Fear is a feeling induced by a perceived threat or danger which causes a change in metabolic and organ functions as well as a change in behavior. Physiologically, fear may manifest as a tightening of muscles, quickness of breath, heaviness in the heart, slowness of the digestive process, dilation of the pupils, contortions in facial muscles etc.

> "Fear is pain arising from the anticipation of evil." –Aristotle

Fear in humans may occur by way of a reaction to a certain stimulus happening in the present or in anticipation/expectation of a future risk. There are *three* possible reactions to fear and one much-needed response. The three possible *reactions* to fear (and anger) are: *fight*, *flight* (both of which are substitutions for a fear), and *freeze* (an unmetabolized experience). So, we:

1. confront through anger
2. flee through avoidance
3. become rooted to the spot in paralysis

The (rational) *response* is to *face* our fears. An irrational fear is a phobia. So, we need to **Face Everything And Rise** rather than **Forget Everything And Run**. For the more you flee from your fears, the more they follow you.

The harsh truth is this: You are the cause *not* of what happens to you but how you choose to respond to what happens to you. You choose how you're feeling. The responsibility rests with you.

> "Men are disturbed not by things, but by the views which they take of things." –Epictetus

Our inner *attitude* to the event is what matters more so than the event itself. We may call this the **ABC** code: **A**void casting **B**lame on external factors outside your **C**ontrol. It's all about your Attitude, Behavior, and Choices in life.

"Some things are in your control and others not." –Epictetus

"If you wish not to be irascible, do not feed your habit; put before it nothing which will make it grow. As the first step, keep quiet and count the (consecutive) days on which you have not been angry." –Epictetus

Two Types of Fear

Fear is the great enemy. It disturbs our peace and harmony, sucks our vitality and energy, drains our nervous system. There are *two* kinds of fear:

1. Rational or natural fear—where there is a threatening situation.
2. Irrational or unnatural fear—which has no objective reality (a phobia, for example).

The origin of most neurotic fears (number two above) can be traced back to childhood, where seeds lie dormant in the unconscious mind and sprout forth in times of stress and strain.

Effects of Fear

Anxiety and worry are the effects of fear. Once fear is dispelled, the person will know peace. What we might call 'normal' fear is healthy as it preserves life. Absolute fearlessness is possible even though psychologists who have had no transcendental experience will deny this. Fear exists where there is duality. Non-duality creates fearlessness. *Fortitude is required in the face of fear*. For Aristotle, courage (or fortitude) is the mid-point between an excess (rashness) and a deficiency (cowardice). This is the doctrine of the Golden Mean in Aristotelian ethics. It's not that the courageous person will feel no fear, as we said earlier. It's just that he will be in right relationship with it. So: muster courage, draw strength from within, move forward courageously and look not back. These are the wise words from Sri Swami Sivananda, a medic and monastic, in his little book, *Conquest of Fear*, the main points of which I will summarize below. He argues that we are born for higher things, so we need to shake off faintheartedness and be bold and cheerful. Sattvic (*sattva* is a mode of existence or quality of being, suggestive of serenity and peace) courage is born of the Self, as is synchronicity. Fear exists to show courage. As calamities occur all around us, we need to cultivate the virtue of courage, which will sustain us during times of trial and tribulation. Just like the rock on the seashore is not touched by the dashing waves, so neither is the Self affected by fear. The Self can smile away all dangers, discord, difficulties and disappointments. He encourages us to:

- Be good
- Serve
- Love
- Give
- Meditate

And nothing will frighten you; even death will hold no terror for you. Above all, don't terrify yourself with imaginary fears. In *Julius Caesar* (2.2.32–37), Shakespeare observes:

> Cowards die many times before their deaths;
>
> The valiant never taste of death but once.
>
> Of all the wonders that I yet have heard,
>
> It seems to me most strange that men should fear;
>
> Seeing that death, a necessary end,
>
> Will come when it will come.

Cowards die many times before their deaths because their fears expose them to danger. So:

- Be bold
- Be cheerful
- Have faith

As an emotion, fear can produce the following physiological effects on/in the person:

- Pallor of the face
- Palpitation of the heart
- Slowing of the pulse
- Tremor of the limbs
- Perspiration

- Expressionless condition of the eyes
- Choking of the voice

The mind is stunned, the senses inhibited. One may even die of shock in extreme cases.

The most common *psychological* fear is the thought that I will end/disappear with the death of my physical body. I then either engage in aggrandizing the body-ego by way of reaction (for example, I might push the body in extreme sports to master it and feel superior) or I play the part of victim. But I cannot equate my entire Self with my body. The thought that accompanies the feeling is this one: 'I am my gross body.' The 'cure' is the recognition that the true 'I' that I am, is eternal, ageless, imperishable. We need to abide in the awareness of this truth/realization. Then I won't mistake myself to be either the body or the mind.

To be free of fear is to face it. The separate self is only a delimitation of the infinite Self. It wants what it doesn't have or dislikes what it has. The ego resists that which is. Fear is one name we give to this resistance. The ego is tight whereas the Self is like an open space. It neither objects to anything nor gets attached to anything. So, the best way to face your fears is to deprive them of oxygen—not to have truck with them, to give them no agenda. Whenever fear arises, enter the true Self through mantra-based meditation. Practice unattached acceptance of all arisings within one, be they fear or anger. This involves a shift in consciousness, a psychological (even ontological) pivoting or pirouetting. The Self knows no fear, because there is no 'other,' no sense of separation. The ego divides the world into objects and subjects so then we fight or flee from the fear; we escape or eliminate/eradicate, all of which is counterproductive. Living with fear is an activity of the separate self/ego. Always notice with what one is identifying.

Fear can be caused by a perceived threat to the body-mind organism. Such a fear can be:

- Real, or
- Imaginary

"Where fear is, there is your task." –C. G. Jung

Fear operates as a kind of signaling mechanism. The same could be said about anger and anxiety, and other manifestations. However, *the perceived source of the threat is not the cause of the fear*. It's just the way the body-mind has been programmed to react. A person perspires nervously when he mistakenly sees a snake instead of a rope in the semi-darkness. The fear evaporates immediately he realizes the truth of things. Identify whether the fear has originated as a signal of threat faced by the body or by the (imaginary) ego with its separate sense of selfhood. Notice the fear; let the body take appropriate means in response to the perceived threat which momentarily may mean fight, flight or digging one's heels in.

Self-realization is really the only way to rid oneself of fear. Fear and attachment are modifications in the mind—temporary waves or worldly whirlpools. They are the substance of the mind. Fear and attachment are close cousins. The separate self produces egoism. By contrast, the Self is fearless and ever blissful. In egoic consciousness, fears multiply daily, hourly. *Attachment is the associate of all fear.* Fear and attachment continually co-exist. Where there is attachment, there is fear.

Examples

If I identify with or attach to my body, then I will fear aging and death.

If I attach to my partner, then I will fear losing him/her.

If I attach to my beautiful possessions such as a house or car, then I will fear being dispossessed of these objects of desire.

So, in pleasure, there is the fear of pain.

In sensual indulgence, there is the fear of disease.

In a good job or position in society, there is the fear of disgrace or fall from status.

In wealth, there is the fear of poverty.

In beauty, there is the fear of ugliness.

In learning, there is the fear of someone being a better scholar.

In the human body, there is the fear of death (the greatest existential dread).

BUT: *if there is no attachment, there is no fear.*

Attachment to or egoic-identification with one's own body is the fundamental or foundational fear. It's the one from which all others derive. It's the first link in the chain. He who is free from attachment is free from fear—and anger. *In non-attachment, there is fearlessness.*

Perhaps fear is not a natural or necessary instinct required for survival but a socially acquired trait arising out of the idea of losing something we have and think we own (is ours by right). A slight deviation or distraction from the Self can cause fear, because it diminishes the stature of the witnessing Self.

In Plato's dialogue, the *Phaedo*, we see Socrates speaking to his upset friends before his execution by hemlock. He believes he knows the secret: "No evil can ever possibly happen to a good man, in this world or the next."[5] This man who said he knew nothing, seems now certain that one thing is needed: to be good, and in the light of moral goodness all fear vanishes. This man who was about to leave life and exit from the stage, then says this: "To fear death is to appear to be unwise without being so; for it is to appear to know what one does not know."[6] Perhaps death is the very best thing.

"In the moral life the enemy is the fat relentless ego." –Iris Murdoch

Causes of Fear: The Three Is

Ignorance is the cause of fear.

Identification is the cause of fear.

Inferiority (feelings of) *is another cause of fear.*

Humans tasted of the forbidden fruit and forgot their original divine nature, caught up, as we were, in ignorance. We felt shame on assuming ourselves were our bodies ("Adam" and "Eve" then covered themselves up with fig leaves)—all this according to the (symbolic) myth (*mythos* = sacred story) of Genesis, which details the evolution of reflective self-consciousness. And so, finite fear entered the realm. (Parenthetically, so-called "Original" Sin only came after Original Innocence [Eden], and of the God who "saw that it was good," indeed "very good").

---

5. Plato, *Apology*, 41d.
6. Plato, *Apology*, 29a.

The Nine Faces of Fear

Fear and Attachment

Fear (*Bhaya*) and attachment (*Raya*) are twin sisters. So, if we attach or identify with the body, with bones and blood, we become timid people with all sorts of little fears. Such an egoic life is mean-minded and narrow, crooked, if you will. Sivananda calls it a "pig-philosophy." Attachment—clinging and cleaving—to the body and earthly life is the cause of most fear. To spell it out and repeat: *attachment to objects causes fear*. Abandon attachment and fear will vanish all by itself. As we know, we become attached to all sorts of things from pens to people, from books to beds. And fear creeps in because we fear losing what we have. Fears fan the flames of jealousy and greed and anger and soon we are agitated in all sorts of ways. In short, man becomes a monkey. The person becomes a prisoner or a puppet.

> "Unhappiness is caused by fears, or by endless and empty desires; but he who is able to rein these in creates for himself a blissful understanding." –Epicurus

Examples

From exam fear to stage fright, one may actually contract that which one fears, so that the bright student who has studied hard and is well prepared goes into an exam with the sudden prospect of failing and sure enough he does. *Fear brings about that which it fears*. We torment ourselves thus: "What will happen if I get lost getting there?" "What will happen if my business venture fails?" There is no end to such imaginary fears. What a way to live. So: sit for a while and introspect. Watch your fears take to their heels. The mischievous mind will deceive you with imaginary fears, therefore:

- Learn to discriminate
- Cogitate
- Reflect
- Cultivate courage
- Be a silent witness to the mind's menagerie

Phobias

Phobias are peculiar, private, irrational fears. Some phobic persons are afraid of snakes, others of snails; some are afraid of clowns, others of crowds; some are afraid of sleeping alone while others are afraid of the dark. Some people are afraid of whole nations; others are afraid of everything. Phobias are endless. Sivananda suggests that the causes of phobias are nervousness, mild to intense stupidity, and lack of enquiry/right thinking and understanding. Again here, it's important to develop firmness, resilience, and the power of resistance.

Exposure Therapy

Slowly seek to move into that which you fear. For example, if you fear multitudes, move slowly into the company of crowds, staying calm. If you're afraid of the dark, take a torch on a walk in the night, then try to walk a little without any light. Because fear is a negative force, it can't stand a positive force like courage. One may have to consult a sage (teacher) or a shrink (therapist). Why are we afraid? Because we love certain things and become attached. *Love is the cause of fear.* We don't want to part with things, even if they are perishable. The remedy is renunciation.

Practical Parenting

Parents often frighten children by their stories, for example, telling them the bogey man is going to get them or singing certain verses to them, one of which goes:

> "Three blind mice.
> Three blind mice.
> See how they run.
> See how they run.
> They all ran after the farmer's wife,
> Who cut off their tails with a carving knife,
> Did you ever see such a sight in your life,
> As three blind mice?"

Some are far worse! These fears coalesce in the subconscious minds of small children, and become deeply implanted there, producing in some cases a complex. The mind of a child is malleable, plastic, and impressionable. So, be careful what you teach children. Why tell them stories that will frighten them? Sivananda likens the mind to a camera plate. Whatever is exposed to the lens is registered and permanently impressed on the mind-plate. Rather, read stories of courage to your children. Tell them they have nothing to fear. It's only the child's imagination which creates the sensation of fear within. Make sages or saints of them, not nervous wrecks. The destiny of the world is in the hands of intelligent mothers, mainly.

Forms of Fear

Fear depletes energy, exhausts. No-one is absolutely free from fear except the complete sage as he sees his own Self everywhere. Fear assumes different forms. For example, a soldier is not afraid of a knife or a bullet but may be afraid of a mouse. A hunter is not afraid of a tiger or rifle but may fear a surgeon's scalpel. The ruler will be afraid of his enemies, the beautiful woman of old age. The frog is afraid of the snake just as the cobra is afraid of the mongoose.

Degrees of Fear

There is being startled, simple fright, shyness, timidity, alarm, panic, terror. Where there is terrible fear, urine and fecal matter may be somatically discharged. What can be done when in the grip of fear? The Jesuits have a saying: "*agere contra*" ("act against"), in other words, do the opposite. It's close to Viktor Frankl's therapeutic technique of 'paradoxical intention.' Desire to have happen the thing you fear most. Repeating a mantra in the mind is one option; simply say 'be courageous now.' According to this formulation of Sivananda's (and I follow his words closely):

- A word is the center of an *idea*.
- An idea is the center of a mental *image*.
- A mental image is the center of a mental *habit*.
- A mental habit is the center of a person's *trait*.

So, have a clear-cut image in the mind of a quality of courage and it will develop. The "will" will come to your aid. *Desire* to be courageous and the "will" will follow, for the "will" is nothing other than rational desire. The most powerful method by which to dispel fear is to identify with the Self. Self-surrender. When fear is removed, nothing can hurt or harm you.

Triumph over Fear

Fear is a universal instinct which can happen at any time. It prevails among insects and animals. It's generally the result of some superior force or power imposing itself on you. Liberation from the objects of fear is needed in order to feel no fear. One shouldn't confuse fear with being suddenly startled. Overcome dualism; develop cosmic love, for where there is love there is no enmity. Feel the unity of everything—the oneness of all. There is no second thing. Fear cannot and does not emanate from one's Self.

Practice facing the fear. And re: approaching sleep, one should never go to bed in a state of fear or worry or brooding. Evacuate such thoughts. Be at peace. Dwell upon divine thoughts. Remain in the higher stratum of mind. As you think, so you will become. Thought is transformational. So, say: "I am all courage." Place the seeds of courage in your heart. Allow it to grow there and fear will die by itself. This is an immutable psychological law: the positive always overcomes the negative. Love and hate are not evenly balanced. Hate is not the equal opposite of love, as love has no opposite. To illustrate this: you can't have a lie without the truth (a lie presupposes the existence of truth) but you can have truth without a lie. The lie is dependent on truth, is parasitic but Truth exists independently. To sum up:

1. Cultivate courage
2. Repeat a meditation mantra in the mind
3. Think on the opposite

The wandering mind has to be wound up, according to Sivananda, by the triple cord of:

1. Devotion
2. Concentration
3. Meditation

Try to spend some time alone each day even if only for a few minutes. Occupy your leisure time well. Select a lonely place—this could be a meadow, a mountain, a riverbank, the terrace of your house or the corner of a church: purge all wavering thoughts. Sitting still will help. Perhaps light a candle or

The Nine Faces of Fear

burn some incense sticks. Steady the mind by gazing at a particular spot or icon and utter slowly (Sivananda's advice):

"God-is-now-here" ("God is nowhere").

- Relax
- Repeat
- Recognize
- Realize

Say:

"His presence is joy."

"His presence is love."

"His presence is peace."

Your mind will come around. This practice will free you from fear. Devotion to the transcendent-immanent Absolute eradicates all fear. Your cup of poison can be transformed into nectar. Finally, fortitude will replace fear. A sage neither hates not fears. A sage beholds the fearless Self only everywhere! Then: who is to be afraid of whom? Abide in the shade and shelter of the Almighty. "He restoreth my soul: he leadeth me in the paths of righteousness for his name's sake. Yea, though I walk through the valley of the shadow of death, I will fear no evil: for thou art with me; thy rod and thy staff they comfort me" (Ps 23:1–4 KJV).

We said above that fear can be a reaction to danger, but dangers can come from outside as well as inside. Freedom from fear is twofold: we must train to circumscribe the present moment and to realize we are not our bodies (which die). We (our essence) does not dissolve into nothingness.

"Fear keeps us focused on the past or worried about the future."
–Thich Nhat Hanh

In China and Vietnam, they call the womb, "the palace of the child." But with birth, the baby is thrust out into an alien world; it's cold and hungry and sounds are too loud for it and lights are too bright. The baby feels fear. For the first time it's afraid of something. This is *original fear*. The umbilical cord is cut, and the separate self is born. So, fear comes into the world with birth, along with the desire to survive, which is the *original desire*. Thus, these *two*: fear and survival. When we grow up, our original fear and desire are still with us, but covered over. We fear we cannot survive the grueling in court, the breakup, moving to a new house, the loss of a loved one, etc. We fear no-one will care for us. Every desire and every fear are rooted in the foundational fear and the foundational desire. All fear—the fear of loneliness, sickness, old age, dying—is the result of the first fear.

> "That original fear—and its other face, original desire—is always there. The infant, with his fear and his desire, is always alive in us."
> –Thich Nhat Hanh

This means that we need to look closely to identify the *primal fear* and *primal desire* behind our behavior because all fear and all desire are a continuation of the original ones. We will explore this more fully when we come to the Enneagram system.

In *Fear*, Thich Nhat Hanh, the well-known Zen Buddhist, makes the persuasive point that our umbilical cord ties us to rivers (through the water we drink), forests (where trees create oxygen for us to breathe), and farmers (who grow the food we eat). Everything is interconnected. Everything links up in the great chain/web of being.

We tend to dwell/fixate on the past and worry about the future, which is nothing other than a projection of both fear and desire from the past. We replay old memories and events that continue to cause us to suffer, or we react to new events as if they were old ones. Rather than looking at things freshly (as Irish poet Patrick Kavanagh put it in "Advent," with "the newness that was in every stale thing, when we look at it as children") we let ourselves become fearful, fragile and forlorn. We have "tested and tasted too much" as weary adults and fail to see the wonder of creation through a child's eyes. We need to "charm back the luxury of a child's soul," "the spirit-shocking wonder" of it all, from "bog-hoes, cart-tracks, old stables" to "wherever life pours ordinary plenty" because "Christ comes with a January flower." If we could only operate in the present moment like a child and be anchored there, then we could really look forward to a future without fear.

Ancestral fears have been transmitted to us; they are part and parcel of our genetic heritage, are present in every cell of our body. The greatest fear is dying, leaving "it all" behind. Epicurus's logic is reassuring: "Death is nothing to us. When we exist, death is not; and when death exists, we are not."[7]

Five Remembrances for Fear

Thich Nhat Hanh puts forward *five* remembrances to help with fear:[8]

1. My nature is to grow old.
2. My nature is such that I can't escape having ill health.
3. My nature is such that I am going to die.
4. I am finally going to be separated from everything and everyone I love.
5. I inherit the results of my acts of body, speech and mind. These actions are my continuation (in other words, our fruits follow us).

These five facts are universal, inevitable truths; it would be foolish to fight or flee from. They are ineluctable. There is no escape—they are givens. We usually try to ignore them through frenzied activities or frenetic distractions and busyness. These remembrances help us accept our deepest fears—old age, sickness, separation and dying, as facts we can't elude, facts which can't be gainsaid. He suggests that we bring mindfulness to bear on the seeds of fear.

When mindfulness embraces our fears, the energy of the fear decreases. There are *two* energies present: the energy of the fear and the energy of mindfulness. When we breathe in the present, fears dissipate. Mindfulness—be it in meditation or breathing—is the gift of fearlessness.

"Nonfear is the basis of true happiness." –Thich Nhat Hanh

"Nonfear is the ultimate joy." –Thich Nhat Hanh

Through meditation, we are able to detach, to un-attach and fears dissipate. If we are locked into our separate selves, then we have much to fear; we have great fear. And if you are afraid, you can't be completely happy. If you're still craving and clinging and cleaving and chasing one object of desire after another you will never have happiness because happiness is here, hidden in the unadorned present moment. Happiness is now or it is never.

7. Epicurus, *Letter to Menoeceus*.
8. Hanh, *Fear*, 30.

"The present is free from fear." –Thich Nhat Hanh

"The present alone is our happiness." –Goethe

The Pure Land is the promised land, is the present moment. Freedom from fear is the foundation of lasting happiness.

There are *two* dimensions of reality: the historical or horizontal (our limited lifespan) and the vertical or ultimate (our eternal life). The analogy given is that between wave and water. The wave represents historical consciousness—it seems to have a beginning and an end. The water is the other dimension of the wave. But the wave is always water. When the wave is a wave, it is (also) already water. To give two more examples: a cloud can become rain or hail, but it cannot become nothing. When you burn a sheet of paper, you see it transform into smoke, vapor, ash, and heat; it continues in other forms. So, stop being controlled by fear, especially the fear of death. Imagine being like Socrates before his death. His last words publicly spoken in the courtroom were: "Now it is time that we were going. I to die, and you to live, but which of us has the happier prospect is unknown to anyone but God."[9]

When fearful or angry or anxious or sad, focus on your happiest recollection. Water the seeds of happiness lest they die or other seeds, such as anger, regret, or despair, start to sprout. Mindfulness, which is awareness, with its energy of calm, eases, erases fear. If caught or captured by fear, go to the island within where clarity and calm reign. *Two* rules or recommendations from Thich Nhat Hanh:

1. Stop (practice pausing)
2. Look (become aware)

These two are really one. If the emotion becomes too strong:

1. Breathe mindfully, or
2. Go out for a mindful walk (focus on your footsteps)

The Four Rs

Don't let your mind carry you away from the present. Traverse the *four* Rs:

9. Plato, *Apology*, 42a.

The Nine Faces of Fear

1. Relax (be at peace)
2. Release (all tension)
3. Reduce (the pain)
4. Recognize (the fearful feeling)

Say "hi and bye" to the feeling of fear. Bring your attention downward into your abdomen (practice 'belly breathing'). Shift your center of gravity. When you're het up—either anxious or afraid—the energy is in your chest and neck. So, don't stay there. Remember, emotions are only emotions. It's their nature to come and go. They stay with us for a while before moving on. You're much more than your feelings, aren't you? Furthermore, our fear impacts on others ("the contagion effect"), so we contribute to creating a climate or culture of fear. Wisdom and compassion put out the flames of fear. The unity of heart and mind is the marriage of wisdom with compassion. Freedom from fear involves undoing attachments. Fear can only be really removed with love.

To give this analogy from Thich Nhat Hanh: there's always blue sky somewhere above the clouds, even if storms and clouds and fog clog the blue sky. Heaven is hidden by a veil of ignorance. Fear and anger cover up the blue sky. *It's a cover-up.*

When we feel fear, we can also engage in mantra meditation, which is a kind of magic formula. We can practice *deep listening* and *loving speech*. (Perhaps all meditation is *Metta* which means "loving kindness," meditation). In a way, the practice of mediation is the practice of happiness. When we touch the ultimate dimension of reality, we free ourselves from fear entirely.

"If you can dwell in one moment, you will discover eternity."
–René Char

Insults and How to Deal with Them

We fear being insulted, ignored, disrespected, scoffed at, scorned, abused, abandoned. Insults directed at us can cause intense anger or rage. Insults can range from the benign to the blatant. They cause an instant insult-reflex, and we may wish to retaliate. Words can be used as weapons to criticize or condemn. There is back-biting and back-stabbing, slagging and subtle

What Is Fear? The Alchemy of an Emotion

social digs. Insults give rise to negative emotions, especially anger. Indeed, most anger is triggered by the insults of others which seem to be designed to hurt or humiliate us. Praise is the opposite of an insult.

The Stoics suggest that the best way to respond to an insult is with no response at all. Or, if we are compelled to say something, we should *respond* (not *react*) with humor or with words of insult directed *not* at the person who has insulted us but at ourselves. And the best type of humor to employ is self-deprecating humor (or "self-defeating" humor as I heard one person describe it!). We need a strategy, therefore. There are *twelve* possible ways to respond to an insult:

1. Avoid other people (not practical in the long run)
2. Avoid individuals who are insulting (hard in the long run)
3. Attack back: Retaliate with a counter-insult (anger as a sign of weakness)
4. Ignore such insulting individuals (difficult but not impossible)
5. Capitulate to the insult (this is giving ground and ceding control to the other, which is not advisable)
6. Respond with humor (a witty comeback is one of the best ways of dealing with insults)
7. Insult ourselves more (this stops the insulter in his tracks and baffles them)
8. Dismiss the insult by transforming it into a joke ("dereflection" through humor)
9. Respond with gratitude (say, "Thanks")
10. Shrug it off (dismiss it; say, "Sorry, I don't do insults." Or meet an insult with silence).
11. Analyze the insulter (ask, "Are you in a bad mood?" or "Why would you say that?" A more aggressive response would be "Whatever," or "What makes you think I care what you think about me?")
12. Agree with the insulter ("What you say is, sadly, true"). An example: "Your nose is big." "Big? It's huge."

The main thing is to refuse verbal violence. Prefer playful teasing instead. "Insult pacifism" is the Stoic default response to every insult. The person who insults you wants a risible reaction, so don't give him what he wants.

The Nine Faces of Fear

The Stoics have a two-pronged approach to dealing with insults. *Two* factors need to be worked on: your *external response* (one of the twelve listed above) and your *internal response* (this concerns the *attitude* you adopt to the situation which should be based, for the Stoics, on "indifference," i.e., not caring what other people say or think about you, as long as you are living according to virtue and values). Know that always somebody will be insulted by something you (unintentionally) do or say.

The external response should be to remain calm and in control while the inner response should be to remain detached and not to put store on social status, thus preventing an insult from upsetting you or sticking to you. Gain *immunity* from insults. Act as if the insult is insignificant (because it is) against the cosmic scheme of things. Life is too short to get worked up over other people's jabs, barbed comments and bad behavior.

Perhaps they're revealing some truth about yourself which could be worth considering. So, be thankful! But know they don't have the power to make you unhappy. That's up to you. You are the key to your own happiness.

Inure yourself to insults. Play a different game with all those people who will scream, shout and insult you. Do you want to care that much about them that you will even enter the orbit of their personality and their toxic emotions? Stay clear. Protect your Self. Love from a distance. Epictetus: "Remember that it is not he who gives abuse or blows, who affronts, but the view we take of these things as insulting."[10] They can only harm you if you let them. The person who insults you should provoke your pity rather than your rage. Seek to become free of fear and anger.

"A gentleman never insults anyone unintentionally." –Oscar Wilde

So, become impassive to insults. Practice the external Stoic strategy of *insult pacifism* and the internal one of *self-transformation* (modification of attitude, as it is called in logotherapy). *Two* things will happen:

1. You will succeed in frustrating your insulter.
2. You will prevent yourself from getting upset/annoyed over an insult that might otherwise ruin your day.

Whether it be through distraction, dereflection or detachment, you don't want fear or anger to take hold of you or take root within you, for it might make a home there. We thus need to monitor our emotions and pay

---

10. Epictetus, *The Enchiridion*, 20.

attention to our feelings and thoughts. Aim at progress not perfection, at incremental self-improvements. Seneca: "[R]equire not from me that I should be equal to the best, but that I should be better than the wicked. It is enough for me if every day I reduce the number of my vices."[11] It's just likely that such people will become good.

Some Examples of Witty Repartees:

Actress Ilka Chase's response to Humphrey Bogart when, after telling her how much he had enjoyed her most recent book, he asked "By the way, who wrote it for you?" was "I'm so glad you liked it. By the way, who read it to you?"

In a second-hand bookstore George Bernard Shaw came across a copy of a book of his, which he had given to a friend. The inscription had read: "With esteem, George Bernard Shaw." He purchased the book and made a small correction, sending it off once more: "With renewed esteem, George Bernard Shaw."

When Theodore Roosevelt was in London, Kaiser Wilhelm II invited him to visit him the next day. He was instructed by note: "Be there at two o'clock sharp, for I can only give you forty-five minutes." Roosevelt replied: "I'll be there at two o'clock sharp, but unfortunately I have just twenty minutes to give you."

George Bernard Shaw once sent Sir Winston Churchill two tickets for the opening night performance of one of his plays with a note that said: "bring a friend—if you have one." Churchill said he was busy that evening, but could Shaw send him tickets for the second performance—if there was one!

Nancy Astor to Churchill: "Winston, if I were married to you, I'd put poison in your tea." Churchill: "Nancy, if you were my wife, I'd drink it."

Churchill's response to politician Bessie Braddock who scolded Sir Winston for being drunk: "Indeed madam, and you are ugly, but tomorrow I'll be sober."

Finally, Gore Vidal once insulted Norman Mailer's writing. Mailer had responded by punching Vidal. As Gore got up from the floor he commented: "Once again, words have failed you Norman."

---

11. Seneca, *Of a Happy Life*, 17.

Tyrants of the Soul

In the *Republic*, Plato named *six* tyrants operating within the person: anger, fear, jealousy, desire, pleasure, and pain. *Anger is caused by the frustration of desire.* So, when anger arises in your heart, ask: "What desire is being frustrated now?" and "Is it a reasonable desire?" See what effect on your anger asking these questions has.

In the *Laws*, Plato argues that it is an injustice when anger, fear, pleasure, or desire tyrannize the soul: Justice, for Plato, by contrast, is inner harmony.

> "The tyranny imposed on the soul by anger, or fear, or lust, or pain, or envy, or desire, I generally call 'injustice.'" –Plato

We have the mistaken belief that the fulfilment of desire leads to happiness. It doesn't. It just leaves us wanting more. This is the nature of desire. Desire attaches to objects and leaves us wanting. Desires enter the heart of humans first as guests then as hosts until they become masters and we become enslaved by desires. If objects of desire don't produce happiness, what does? The answer cannot be in doubt: desirelessness. All we need to do is drop the desire and the fear or the anger will dissipate. With desirelessness, there is no discontent. Desires proliferate, producing much misery. Desire is (mainly) the eternal foe, not the friend.

All Anger Is Frustrated Desire

The key is to practice detachment, to let go or surrender, to become the seer/observer of your own life—witness it and respond to need alone. Also, increase the gap between a stimulus and a response, enlarging the interval between desires. Drop into stillness and the fear or the anger will dissolve. Release leads to peace. It's our *attachment* to desires that's the problem more than the desires themselves, to put it more accurately.

Fear and Anger

Anger is the root cause of so many physical and mental health problems. It's linked to increased possibility of stroke, heart disease, and cancer; it also impairs decision-making and our relationships with others. If it causes so many destructive things, we need to focus on the cure. One in three people can't control their temper. They reach boiling point and lose the head (reason). One in four people battle with anger problems. Almost anything can trigger anger, from mild irritations such as losing one's car keys and traffic jams to cruel words or acts of violence that beget even more anger. One thing you will find: anger usually always escalates.

Hostility (aggression) builds up when love is frustrated. Indeed, anger is not possible without love. Love under attachment produces frustration and therefore anger. There is a gap between the way I'd like things to be, and the way things actually are. This gap causes anger. But who creates the gap? Me! We thus arrive at the awful truth: *I make myself angry. I am the cause of my own anger.* The opposite of anger: *acceptance*. But who do we think makes us angry? Everyone else! The stronger my attachment is to things/people, the greater will be the power of my anger towards them when my ego desires are not being met. Putting that another way: the degree of attachment determines the level of (my) anger—and my fear. The fatal belief is that I have no choice in the matter, that the fault resides in the other. When I blame everyone else, I never have to take personal responsibility for my own thoughts, feelings and actions. Anger isn't natural—love is. Fear isn't natural—love is. This is the proposition: *love is the natural in-between.* In other words, when in any situation we are being truly ourselves without obscurity or prejudice or ignorance, then love will be the default setting in all our friendships, encounters, and conversations.

If anger persists, what can I do? Let's see the options again: I can let off steam by venting anger. The problem here is that we're still practicing anger and, in fact, we're strengthening anger. Or I can repress it. But the problem here is that the anger continues to bubble and burn away and will re-ignite at a later stage. The third way beyond the dualism of express or repress is to dissolve anger. We can do this through the proper use of reason; here we ask ourselves: "what's the point in being unhappy/angry/fearful?" We can practice meditation which stills the heart. We can draw on wisdom (philosophy) and realize/understand the true nature of my anger (and my fear). This would mean recognizing that I am the cause of it, and I am therefore the cure of it, that others are not responsible for how I feel, that anger is not a true emotion, and that I need to accept that which is. The prize is peace. Anger is a parasite. Reactions are instinctual and mechanical. So too is habit. Love isn't. Love is intentional rather than instinctual; it's responsive rather than reactive. The more we love, the less we fear and the less we are angry. If we are really present to ourselves, we can spot these impostors coming. So, catch it early and head it off. Give it no energy. Not reacting does not reinforce anger, it dissolves it. For that, we need to be awake and attend to the present moment. To want to change everybody else is not heroism, it's ignorance. It's not enlightenment, it's ego. The difference is between "Heaven" (happiness accruing from love) or "Hell" (suffering deriving from fear and anger). The choice is ours.

Anger doesn't change the world, "righteous" anger so-called including —only love does that. Anger separates, love unites. You can't be angry or fearful and happy at the same time. Just ask yourself: what type of person do you really want to be? And make the change. Love, not anger, is the natural in-between. And if love is not the natural in-between, what is?

Fear and Anxiety

Fear is closely related to anxiety. The difference between fear and anxiety is that anxiety is perceived to be more uncontrollable or unavoidable. Anxiety is diffuse and generic; it spreads out. Fear is specific; it latches onto, attaches to an object. Fear may be uncertain but it's not indefinite. Fear of the known is depression; fear of the unknown is anxiety.

We looked at anger briefly above, let's try now to offer an answer to anxiety. Anxiety tends to focus on the future. The anxious person will worry and engage in negative thought-patterns so the two most important things to do is to stop thinking and be in the present. How do you do this? By meditating. Repeat a mantra. Still your mind. What follows are *three* steps:

1. Check in with the present moment. Ground yourself in the meaning of the moment. The present instant is not causing you any stress— your thinking is. So, focus your attention on the sensations of your breathing—on sounds and colors.

2. Lay out the outcomes of what you're worried about in a journal. Ask: what do you think will happen? What evidence (past experience) have you that the outcome you're worried about will actually occur? Is there any evidence that it won't happen?

3. Ask: is this fear/worry/anxiety doing you any good right now? Is it helping or hindering? Put it to the side; park it.

So, meditate, write, and employ right reason as you engage in Self-enquiry. To put it another way: Obey the imperative of the instant; dereflect (in other words, put your mind/thoughts on positive things); and weigh the

What Is Fear? The Alchemy of an Emotion

evidence for and against your worrying—see other possible outcomes to your anticipations. Don't assent to anxiety. Stay CALM:

C: Cognition, also Control. It's about what you think and what you can control. Let go of all those things you can't control. Focus on what's in your power to change—your thoughts and actions.

A: Act. If you can control the situation, then do something about it (with the above advice). If you can't, then:

L: Let go. Find a way to accept what's happening, without causing you anxiety.

M: Move on. Don't dwell on the things outside your control or on negative/toxic thoughts.

Physiological changes in the body that are associated with fear include: accelerated breathing (hyperventilation), increased heart rate, constriction of the peripheral blood vessels leading to blushing, increased muscle tension, including to those attached to hair follicles causing "goose bumps," sweating, hyper-glycemia, butterflies in the stomach, etc. We develop fears as a result of learning. One example of such "fear conditioning" is the "Little Albert" experiment in 1920 which was inspired after observing an eleven-month-old boy with an irrational fear of dogs. He was conditioned (in the Pavlovian sense) to fear a white rat in the laboratory and this fear then became generalized to include other white, furry objects such as a dog and a rabbit and even a cotton-ball. Fear can be learned by watching a traumatic accident so, to give an example, a child who falls into a well might develop a fear of enclosed spaces (claustrophobia) or even water (aquaphobia). The amygdala is affected. People who have damaged their amygdalae are unable to experience fear. Psychopaths are regarded as people who experience a lack of fear as well.

Fear is also affected by cultural and historical contexts. The capacity to feel fear is also part of human nature. Studies have shown that certain fears, like the fear of animals and heights, are more common than others such as the fear of flowers and clouds, which could be the result of natural selection. Seen in the light of our evolutionary heritage, fear could be a different adaptation that has proved useful for our survival as a species.

A 2005 Gallup Poll in the United States asked a sample of adolescents between the ages of thirteen and seventeen what they feared most. The top *ten* fears were: terrorist attacks, spiders, death, failure, war, criminal (or gang) violence, being alone, the future, and nuclear war. In 2008, the most frequent response to the phrase "fear of . . ." was: flying, heights, clowns, intimacy, death, rejection, people, snakes, failure, and driving.[12] For fear to make sense it must meet *three* conditions:

1. The object of fear needs to be "something bad"
2. There needs to be a non-negligible chance that the bad state of affairs will transpire
3. There needs to be some uncertainty about the bad state of affairs

If these three criteria are not met, fear is deemed to be an *inappropriate* reaction. Fear of the unknown is caused by negative thinking (worry) which arises from anxiety, accompanied by a subjective sense of dread. Chronic, irrational fears can be extremely deleterious to one's physical and psychological (mental) health. One would imagine that there is more fear present in those who are geographically placed in war-ridden areas. Poor parenting can likewise instill fear in a child's psyche which can debilitate the person in question, which we touched on above. Developing calm and equanimity (resilience too) to handle fear-provoking situations is advocated as an antidote and has been suggested by a number of ancient philosophers. Fear of the Unknown (FOTU) may just be the fundamental fear, more so than the Fear of Missing Out (FOMO).

Unlike boredom, fear is an intense experience. Indeed, fear is one cure for boredom; curiosity is another. In threatening situations involving some insects and mammals, birds and reptiles, certain chemical alarm signals can be emitted (fear pheromones) to inform others of the same species of the danger. In terms of psychology and therapeutic management, Viktor Frankl's school of logotherapy, offers impressively high clinical success rates. Whatever treatment modality is employed, few would disagree with the premise that facing into fears is the best approach for long-term life efficacy and sustainable happiness.

Questions for Consideration

- How *reactive* would you say you are?
- Do you *face* your fears rather than fighting or fleeing them?

---

12. Lyons, "What Frightens America's Youth?"

- Ask yourself: "Do I really want to become *free* of this particular fear or feeling?"

The Practice

- Try choosing not to be afraid (or angry) in any given situation.
- Become aware of the *story* you add to the event, and of the interpretation you give it.
- Let the fear(s) and anger dissolve in the present moment.
- Ask yourself: "Can I change what I am feeling/fearing right *now*?"
- Observe the effects of fear as well as anger and anxiety on you.
- Meditate daily.
- Begin to practice non-attachment.
- Try not to identify with your emotions.
- Cultivate the virtue of courage.
- Recall the five facts of fear.

2

Formulations on Fear

Don't Avoid Your Fears

> "Avoiding danger is no safer in the long run than outright exposure. The fearful are caught as often as the bold." –Helen Keller

AVOIDANCE IS FUTILE BECAUSE you cannot keep running from yourself. Very often, fear is the assumption of an upcoming calamity or catastrophe. Fear creates stress. Our bodies react producing cortisol (and adrenaline). Fear and anger have extremely similar biochemical responses. Whatever we repress, suppress or block out will return and repeat. We may formulate this as a psychological law thus:

What Resists, Persists.

Resistance is the fuel and fire of fear. The fight against fear causes fear. Do you avoid what you fear? If so, you need to confront your fears head on but step by step. Try and wish to have happen (if only momentarily) the thing you fear most so that the (pathogenic) fear is replaced by a (paradoxical) wish. So, don't react, act; don't resist, accept; don't control, dissolve.

> "Do the thing we fear, and death of fear is certain."
> –Ralph Waldo Emerson

Formulations on Fear

For fears need to be faced. And faced down. The fear-factor is everywhere. Anything can conceivably cause fear, from cats to cages. Frequently, there is some gap or disparity between the person and the object of their fear so that **FEAR** can stand for False Evidence Appearing Real. For example, does it make any logical sense for a grown man to be afraid of a small spider? This little creature has assumed a huge size in the person's mind which is not in accord with the truth of the situation. So, we can say that such a person is not in touch with reality, with that which is. A thought in their mind has intervened and imposed itself on the reality. A schema or construct has intruded so that the person can't see clearly. He is in thrall to this idea (conception) and not to the truth of things (perception).

Your *feelings* of fear represent precisely that—your feelings (all your private, unconscious free-associations) but it doesn't represent the *facts*. **Feelings aren't facts**, as said at the beginning of the book. When we surrender to fear, facts are replaced by fantasy. My mind becomes plagued by "what ifs" and my life becomes cautious and constricted. Very soon I come to inhabit a small space in the world. I don't give all, so I won't lose all. Fear has now gained the upper hand. My life now spins into a constant search for reassurance and appreciation. These are the fruits of fear. So:

Perceive, Don't Conceive.

When the mind takes over the event and adds to it, it conceives rather than perceives. Right reason is displaced by fantasy. A named fear is a concept. Perceiving without conceiving involves *acceptance* of that which is. *There is no emotion or experience independent of our interpretation of it.* Fear is an instrument of perception. The "more" of fear is not just the something we fear—the *physical* object (for example the spider), it's the intentional or *mental* object (how we have construed the spider), which can be reconstrued. It's worth noting that the intentional object doesn't have to be a real object; after all, children are afraid of monsters under their bed. You may *feel* fear, but you *feed* on fear when you focus on the mental object, imbuing it with power over you. To take an example: you get butterflies in your stomach. You feel and experience that. But your mind's conception intrudes and says: "You are going to do badly in this exam." So, just *perceive with conceiving*. Perception takes place in relation to what is. If we take the example of anorexia: the eye might see a thin body, but the mind sees a fat one. Most pain is really non-acceptance. So often we see things in terms of projection or preconceptions—through the prism (prison) of our own assumptions rather than through pure perception. In other words, we don't see the world at all. We view it through a lens, through goggles, and we project our fears through memory (and association) or mere, mechanical habit. Someone might see the rain and say "what a miserable day" but water isn't miserable—there is no misery in rain, only miserable people who get wet by rain. Perhaps this is why Wittgenstein once remarked: "The world of the happy man is different from the world of the unhappy."[1]

Therefore, do not seek to change that which is *outside* your control. Seek only to change that which is *inside* your control, in other words, your own thoughts (attitude/mindset) and actions. And accept the world with all its splendor and suffering just as it is. Ultimately, it's about growing up. To diminish your fear, develop trust in your ability to handle what life throws at you. Aristotle's man of courage, whom we met earlier, still feels fear, but he's not determined by his feelings. Feeling afraid is about not feeling good about yourself. The person of fortitude has freedom to face into his/her fears. He or she may still *feel* their fears, but they don't *fixate* on them. *Whatever we give our attention to, grows.* Be careful so about what you put into your mind.

Questions for Consideration

- Do you avoid your fears?
- Do you worry unduly about the future?
- Do you accept things as they are or seek to change them? If the latter, what things?
- What lens do you see the world through? What pair of glasses are you wearing right now through which you see the world? Are they grey or rose-tinted spectacles?

The Practice

- Try facing into your fears; examine them; expose them to scrutiny like a philosopher might.
- Try doing something you fear even if only momentarily and see how that makes you feel.

1. Wittgenstein, *Tractatus Logico-Philosophicus*, 6.43.

- Try and distinguish between your feelings and fantasies about something on the one hand, and the facts about it, on the other hand.
- Try to just *see* the situation, without adding to what is already there. Simply observe without identifying or attaching.

> "I learned that courage was not the absence of fear, but the triumph over it. The brave man is not he who does not feel afraid, but he who conquers that fear." –Nelson Mandela

Face Facts

> "Present fears are less than horrible imaginings."
> –William Shakespeare

Our minds fabricate fantasies. We create worlds of fiction in our minds—fabulous stories. We are what we think. Therefore, in truth, fear exists only in the mind. *I* am the sole source and cause of my fear (and my anger). All fear originates internally and, therefore, all fear is eliminated from within. Let *four* quotes from the wise guide us:

> "The greatest revolution of our generation is the discovery that human beings, by changing the inner attitudes of their minds, can change the outer aspects of their lives." –William James

> "In its own place the mind can make a heaven of hell or a hell of heaven."
> –John Milton

> "There is nothing either good or bad, but thinking makes it so."
> –William Shakespeare

> "With our thoughts, we make the world." –Buddha

We tell ourselves tall stories such as "I'm not good enough"; "I wouldn't be able to handle that"; "He hasn't texted me in two whole days—he mustn't love me anymore." *These are fantasies not facts.* We need to guard against our inner chatter box—the language we use—because the unconscious believes only what it hears, not what is true. Start paying attention to the language you use about yourself (and other people).

And how do you know you can't handle stuff until it happens? About 90 percent of what we worry about *never happens*. Fear, so, is a projection. If you want to change the world, change the world *you're* in, and how you do that is by changing the way you think about things. We're so busy pre-empting about things in the future, it's no wonder we're full of fear, anxiety, anger and foreboding. The answer to this dilemma is to live in the present. We may put it thus:

Pre-empting Things Is Impossible in the Present.

So, it is in the present that we must live. We can do *two* things here:

1. We can pre-empt the most horrendous things possible by practicing a negative visualization exercise which the Stoics call *praemeditatio malorum* (a premeditation on future evil). Imagine the worst-case scenario. Ask yourself: 'What's the worst possible thing that can happen?' because it's never as bad as you *think*.

2. Concentrate on the meaning of the moment, the call of the hour, the imperative of the instant. Bring your attention to rest in the present rather than anticipating (pre-empting) the future through desire or recalling the past through memory.

Questions for Consideration

- What kinds of things do you give your attention to?
- Do you find yourself pre-empting things?
- What story do you tell about yourself?
- What interests or intrigues you?
- How do you see yourself?

The Practice

- Try silencing the inner chatter box, what St. Benedict calls "murmuring."
- Try to live more in the plenitude of the present moment.
- Bring your thoughts and feelings into the naked Now.

- Just focus on what is taking place in front of you and in you this very minute.

You Are Not Your Fears

"To conquer fear is the beginning of wisdom." –Bertrand Russell

Fear is *not* an objective reflection of reality. Fear is fluid. Fear is a little fact about you—it's not *the* fact about everything. Just as when you have flu, you are not your influenza. It's something you *have*; it's not who you *are*. As we said earlier: You have a body, but you are not (just) your body. You are more than your body. You have a mind, but you are more than your intellect. You have feelings (and sometimes you let your feelings have you) but you are not your emotions because they change and pass just like the snow, just like the storm. What you are in your essence is a center of pure consciousness. This is your Self: large, luminous and limitless.

"There is nothing to fear but fear itself." –Franklin D. Roosevelt

We cannot escape suffering and loss in life. If we fear suffering, we are already suffering from fear. Bad things happen to us all and sometimes good things can come from bad things. Therefore:

"Demand not that things happen as you wish, but wish them
to happen as they do, and you will go on well." –Epictetus

This entails *acceptance* rather than *avoidance*. We may not be able to make fear disappear entirely and forever, but we can diminish, dissipate and dissolve it. The "beyond" of fear is a land of hope and freedom—faith, if you like—faith in the future, *your* future.

The ego is that separate, small self that lives in fear and anger and anxiety. A fearful person is afraid of everything. The fearful person places limits on himself. The ego is limited, bound, contracted, constricted and because of this and the insecurity it brings, it experiences fear. The ego is isolated and because of this feeling of separation, fear and anxiety are produced. The ego is only a fraction of me—perhaps even a fiction, but it is not I myself. The ego is not complete—it's partial and therefore it understands only perspectives. It's biased and prone to seeing things from its own narrow viewpoint. It doesn't see the big picture. The ego is a creature of ignorance and error and craves gain and recognition and fears loss and therefore suffers when its desires are frustrated rather than fulfilled. The ego is capricious, the Self is capacious. So, we need to live from the unbounded Self and not from the the "fat, lying, illusion-making, deceitful ego," as Iris Murdoch calls it, or what Jacques Lacan calls the "monumental construct of man's narcissism."

You don't really need to eliminate fearful objects such as spiders but rather change the person who's afraid of such objects and this happens when you realize that what's fearful about the object is *not the object but the story which you're telling yourself about the object*. Fears arise by what we think we know and that's where they're eliminated from as well.

The mind projects into the future: "What if?" But memory is not knowledge of the future. Projection creates expectation and hope, as well as fear. So, don't anticipate anything. Knowledge of the future is pure fantasy. Fear arises out of false knowledge. What happens when I've no fears? I start to make them up! I think of what *might* happen (and which invariably doesn't happen).

Observe your fears. This is how you detach from them. Spot them to drop them. See that they are not you. Externalize them. Look at your fear in the light of the facts—don't look away. See what is here, NOW, before all conceptions from the past arise. *Let go of the conception. Get back to the perception*. You then become the observing Self—the perceiver of the fear and if you "see" it (in your mind's eye), you can't be it. The false I falls away, and fear is reduced to an object under observation. Know you are not your fear. This is the true use of the mind (intellect) just as acceptance is the proper use of the heart. Both together disarm the fear. Fears shrink when faced.

Questions for Consideration

- Do you find yourself identifying with your feelings or thoughts?
- Do you experience a fear *having you* rather than *you having* the fear?
- Can you distinguish between your clamoring, fearful, anxious or angry ego and your Self which is full and free?

The Practice

- Disidentify from your attachments and identifications.
- Observe your fears as they emerge; see them as objects of your attention.
- Know that you cannot be that which you observe.
- Realize that your fears don't provide you with objective facts about reality—only fables.

Let Go. Detach

"Fear is only as deep as the mind allows." –Japanese Proverb

The person who has nothing to lose is not afraid of anything. Detachment from desire is the key to letting go of fear. Fear is not the problem, we are. We hold onto things and therefore are afraid to lose them. Keep in mind the story of the Monkey Trap which illustrates this point nicely. The only way the monkey can free its hand is to let go of the food and release its grip. What are you holding onto? Are there things you need to let go of? They may be memories or feelings rather than things. What are some of your attachments that are not bringing you happiness or joy anymore? Letting go of them is within your grasp. Sometimes we need to lose in order to gain. Let this paradox be phrased thus:

Abstain in order to Obtain.

One always lets go for more, never for less. Because we are surrendering ego-identifications and attachments in order to live in the bigger house of the Self. If, through my attachments, I over-identify ("hyper-reflect") then the dread of loss will see me fearful. We are guests at the banquet of life: some dishes will be served cold. Say to yourself: "this too passes"; "Let not your heart be troubled"; "*Neti, neti*" ("not this, not this"); "Sufficient unto the day the evil thereof"; "Be still"; "You are just an impression and not at all the thing you claim to represent." This is advice from *three* great schools of thought: Christianity, Vedic philosophy, and Stoicism, respectively. *Ego or let go*. A prayer and a poem may help. The first is the Serenity Prayer by Reinhold Niebuhr.

The Nine Faces of Fear

> God grant me the serenity
> to accept the things I cannot change;
> courage to change the things I can;
> and wisdom to know the difference.

The second is Rudyard Kipling's *If*.

> If you can keep your head when all about you
>   Are losing theirs and blaming it on you,
> If you can trust yourself when all men doubt you,
>   But make allowance for their doubting too;
> If you can wait and not be tired by waiting,
>   Or being lied about, don't deal in lies,
> Or being hated, don't give way to hating,
>   And yet don't look too good, nor talk too wise:
>
> If you can dream—and not make dreams your master;
>   If you can think—and not make thoughts your aim;
> If you can meet with Triumph and Disaster
>   And treat those two impostors just the same;
> If you can bear to hear the truth you've spoken
>   Twisted by knaves to make a trap for fools,
> Or watch the things you gave your life to, broken,
>   And stoop and build 'em up with worn-out tools:
>
> If you can make one heap of all your winnings
>   And risk it on one turn of pitch-and-toss,
> And lose, and start again at your beginnings
>   And never breathe a word about your loss;
> If you can force your heart and nerve and sinew
>   To serve your turn long after they are gone,
> And so, hold on when there is nothing in you
>   Except the Will which says to them: "Hold on!"
>
> If you can talk with crowds and keep your virtue,
>   Or walk with Kings—nor lose the common touch,
> If neither foes nor loving friends can hurt you,
>   If all men count with you, but none too much;
> If you can fill the unforgiving minute
>   With sixty seconds' worth of distance run,
> Yours is the Earth and everything that's in it,
>   And—which is more—you'll be a Man, my son!

Questions for Consideration

- Do you find yourself holding on too tightly in life for fear of loss?
- Can you experience the difference between centered and open attention versus scattered and captured attention?

The Practice

- Notice where you are putting your attention. Let it be open and centered rather than captured or scattered.
- Pause between two desires; put a stop between two actions. Create a gap between a stimulus and a response.
- Act with as much depth and detachment as possible.

"To become fully involved you have to be extremely detached." –Bernard Lonergan, SJ

"He who would be serene and pure needs but one thing, detachment." –Meister Eckhart

Exercises

"The cave you fear to enter holds the treasure you seek."
–Joseph Campbell

Exercise One

Name *three* of your fears, because to name something is to tame it.

1. _____

2. _____

3. _____

The Nine Faces of Fear

Exercise Two

This next exercise, which draws on the Stoic spiritual exercise of *praemeditatio malorum*, is taken from Tim Ferriss (an American entrepreneur). It's about defining your fears instead of your goals and has two parts. In this Fear-Setting Exercise, draw *three* columns, thus:

What if I . . . ?

Define	Prevent	Repair
1.	1.	1.
2.	2.	2.
3.	3.	3.
4.	4.	4.
5.	5.	5.
6.	6.	6.
7.	7.	7.
8.	8.	8.
9.	9.	9.
10.	10.	10.

Under Define, write down whatever your fears are and all those things that cause you anxiety. This is a list of the worst things that you can imagine happening. Under Prevent, write down a list of things that you can do to prevent these fears from happening or decreasing the likelihood of them coming true. Finally, under Repair, assuming that the worst-case scenario has occurred, ask: how can you repair the damage done?

Exercise Three

Ask yourself: If I avoid facing into my fears and anxieties, what might my life look like in six months, one year, three years? List them in *three* columns.

The Cost of Inaction

(Emotionally, Financially, Physically etc).

| 6 months | 1 year | 3 years |

Inaction is not an option.

You might want to rate the above giving 1 to those decisions which would have a minimal impact on you and 10 to describe those with a maximum impact on you.

Questions for Consideration

- Ask yourself: "What's the worst thing that can happen here?"
- Enquire of yourself: "How can I prevent these fears from happening?" "What can I change here about the circumstance or myself?"

Our Threefold Energy

> "The enemy is fear. We think it is hate, but it is fear." –Mahatma Gandhi

Vedic philosophy postulates the existence of *three* energies (*gunah*), which have a single source:

1. Sattva
2. Rajas
3. Tamas

Sattva gives light, knowledge of what needs to be done and well-being. *Rajas* is movement, passion, enthusiasm, creativity. *Tamas* gives refreshment and regulation, brings dissolution. When we meditate, we are in *sattva*—alert, aware, agile; things are clear. We are at ease. Our emotions are uncluttered. *Rajas* ("rage" in English relates etymologically) is energy. *Tamas* occurs when things subside or stop or shut down. *Tamas* conserves. *Tamas* is rest, *Rajas* is action, *Sattva* is awareness.

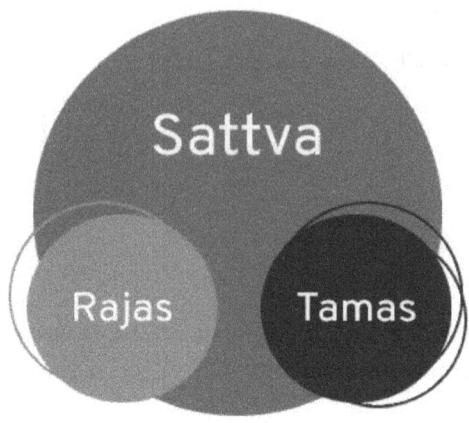

It's about the right measure of energy: there may be underuse, overuse or misuse. *Rajas* can spin out of control as passion turns into anger, for example, or agitation. Too much *Tamas* and we can become lethargic or lazy, catatonic or comatose. With too much *Sattva* (a little unlikely!), we become lost in a dream and live in a bubble. The energies are always present but the balance between them changes. *Sattva* is dawn, *Tamas* is dusk, *Rajas* is daytime. So, we need to pay attention (through the transcendent Self) to our threefold energy field. I may be Rajasic, Sattvic or Tamasic. The observer Self is beyond/independent of the three *gunah*. These energies act on us—on our minds and feelings. So, we need to watch how they operate in and through us.

Rajas is the guna of creation—it's motivation and energy. *Tamas* is the guna of dissolution and death, of sleep and sloth. *Sattva* is the ray of peace and serenity, rest and light. (Matt 11:28–30 NIV: "Come to me, all you who are weary and burdened, and I will give you rest. Take my yoke upon you and learn from me, for I am gentle and humble in heart, and you will find rest for your souls. For my yoke is easy and my burden is light"). Love under *sattva* is pure (agapeic); love distorted under *rajas* is possessive, obsessive; love under *tamas* is *manikon eros*—mad, crazy love (delusional). Happiness is Self-dependent: consolation without cause.

In relation to fear, we become Tamasic when fear arises within us and we freeze (paralysis, postponement, procrastination). We become Rajasic when fear arises within us and we worry and get anxious and become full of perturbation or perplexity. If *rajas* is heavily in the ascendancy there is an excess of energy which can manifest as anger. We become Sattvic when we know no fear and enter into a state of stillness and perpetual peace.

Ultimately, we eliminate fear when we come to know who we are in truth. If I am (just) this body well, then, I am subject to death and "I" cease when my body dies. But if I am (incarnate) spirit, will there be anything really to fear? So, how do we come to know who we are in truth? There are *three* paths:

1. By stilling the mind through *meditation* which connects us with the Self
2. Through the study of *Scripture*(s)
3. Hearkening to the words of the wise (*philosophy*)

We become dominated by everything with which our self is identified. We thus need to dis-identify ourselves. Fear delimits. Put it behind you. It's time to move on and do something about your fears. Isn't it high time we became adults? Children are afraid of the dark because they imagine all kinds of dangers lurking there. But this is the truth: people are NOT afraid of the dark, they're afraid of what they *add* to the dark, through imaginings, false reasoning, fantasies, etc. which are all constructs and conceptions. Just face what's in front of you now and you will fear no evil. If there is joy in gain, there will be fear in loss—this is the law of compensation. So, enjoy it all without delight in gain and fear of loss. Difficult? Yes. Impossible? No. Give over your attention to eternity, to what is unchanging and true (being) rather than to what is ephemeral and transient (becoming). Live out your life from your best Self rather than your base self.

Awaken to your true nature. Abide in the present. Don't dwell on the past or dream of the future. Stay in the open moment of the eternal now where happiness resides. The Maharishi was once asked what he would do if someone ran at him with a knife. He replied: "I'd change my desire."

Questions for Consideration

- Do I practice stillness and inner silence?
- Do I engage in activities mindfully?
- Do I study the words of the wise or read Scripture?
- Do I engage with true reason?

The Practice

- Notice the *three* energies at play within you.
- Try and come into stillness with body, mind, and heart.
- For a period during the day, be in *sattva*.

Fear freezes one into *Tamas* or agitates one into *Rajas*. By contrast, fearlessness prevails in *Sattva*.

Acceptance

> "Of all the liars in the world, sometimes the worst are our own fears."
> –Rudyard Kipling

The answer and antidote to fear lies in acceptance and affirmation, which involves getting up not giving up, and giving of ourselves. Thus, generosity and gratitude, not resignation and despair. It's about living from the expansiveness of the Self. *The answer to fear is learning how to give.* It's about living a life of self-transcendence in loving service to others rather than being incarcerated in our separate selves (hell). For life is ultimately about freedom, not fear. Frankl tells us that there is an intact spiritual core in every (not just) ill person—his/her essence (it goes by different names such as "soul" or "spirit" or "Self"), which cannot be affected or agitated or harmed or become sick or suffer or fear. It is untouched by the creation and by change. As Shakespeare put it in *Cymbeline* (4.2.331–54):

> Fear no more the heat o' the sun,
> Nor the furious winter's rages;
> Thou thy worldly task hast done,
> Home art gone, and ta'en thy wages:
> Golden lads and girls all must,
> As chimney-sweepers, come to dust.
>
> Fear no more the frown o' the great;
> Thou art past the tyrant's stroke;
> Care no more to clothe and eat;
> To thee the reed is as the oak:
> The scepter, learning, physic, must
> All follow this, and come to dust.

> Fear no more the lightning flash,
> Nor the all-dreaded thunder stone;
> Fear not slander, censure rash;
> Thou hast finished joy and moan:
> All lovers young, all lovers must
> Consign to thee, and come to dust.
>
> No exorciser harm thee!
> Nor no witchcraft charm thee!
> Ghost unlaid forbear thee!
> Nothing ill come near thee!
> Quiet consummation have;
> And renownèd be thy grave!

True freedom makes for true happiness. Truth, which we may define as that which is ever the same and doesn't change, we are told, sets us free. So, truth and freedom are one. We all desire to be permanently and not just partially free. I eat to be free of hunger just as I drink to be free of thirst. But just having the desire is insufficient. We need knowledge or wisdom, for many seek fame or fortune, erroneously believing that these represent freedom. The Christian tradition insists that we first seek the Kingdom, and all these other things will be given us. The wise of all ages agree that only the mind of man can be bound and only the mind of man can be free. *Freedom depends on our inner attitude.*

What binds the mind is past knowledge—our feelings, thoughts, preconceptions, prejudices. We then become prisoners of our thoughts. Meanwhile, there have been other prisoners such as Nelson Mandela, Viktor Frankl, Etty Hillesum, who have been free while incarcerated. *We create our own cages.* And nobody can release us except ourselves.

What stops us from becoming free is *ignorance* (the opposite of true reason) and *inequality* (the opposite of real unity). But love transcends all forms and permits us to see into the soul of things, the substance. The third barrier to freedom is *desire*. There can be no full satisfaction of desire. The desired object, once attained, increases the desire for more, as we said above. Limited things in finite time provide only limited amounts of freedom and therefore limited amounts of happiness. The effect of such desire is fear of losing one's possessions, misery at not gaining what one desires or anger when 'my stuff' is taken from me. We're possessed by our possessions. Desires thus narrow our lives, constricting us, overruling even reason. Desires distort and hold us captive. They always come at a cost. *We become bound by that which we desire*. And being bound is bondage. Only one desire expands us, draws us, and that is the desire for freedom.

Externally, we need to realize the profound truth of interdependency, that no man is an island cut off from the main. And internally, we need to feed the *body* with right measure (not too much food, not too little, not too much sleep, not too little etc); the *mind* with right reason (which purifies it) and the *heart* with love (which cleanses it), *not with feelings*. Loving that which is good and deploying reason to discover the truth brings us freedom and happiness. When we love, there is no fear, nor is there any anger. There is only joy.

True freedom is the expanse within one—it's one's inner world or spirit. Absolute freedom would mean living in spirit, therefore. Freedom is available to us all of the time (the good news) but not availed of (the bad news). So how can we attain such freedom? By realizing this truth: that freedom is *never* in the past nor in the future. It is only in the *now*. In fact, we're only truly free in the present.

Questions for Consideration

- Do I practice gratitude each day?
- How do you experience and express it?
- How would you describe your mindset as you meet each day?
- Do you affirm all of life?
- How generous are you with others in terms of sharing what you have (it could be your time) and who you are? (generosity and gratitude are linked)
- Do you live in the present? Where are your thoughts? Do you bring the past into your present?
- How free are you, in truth?

The Practice

- Count your blessings—name *three* things for which you are grateful daily. Keep a Gratitude Diary.
- Observe the effects of gratitude.

- Meet your friends and family members as if for the first time (thus avoiding pre-empting and past 'knowledge').

"The whole secret of existence is to have no fear."
–Swami Vivekananda

Five Forms of Fear and Fifteen Propositions

"Who sees all beings in his own self, and his own self in all beings, loses all fear." –Upanishads

Roberto Assagioli was much influenced by Plato and Advaita. In *Transpersonal Development*, he dedicates chapter fifteen to fear, which he describes as an emotional obstacle to spiritual development.

"I think we would be justified in saying that most of the ills and suffering afflicting humanity are a result of fear." –Roberto Assagioli

Forms of Fear

Fear is like Proteus—it can assume many forms and faces. Fear creates inner suffering. According to Assagioli, there are *five* main forms of fear, which underlie the five fundamental instincts:[2]

1. The instinct of self-preservation, the root of which is the fear of death.
2. The sexual drive, the root of which is the fear of loneliness.
3. The herd instinct, the root of which is the fear of being separated.
4. The tendency to affirm oneself, the root of which is the fear of not being appreciated or recognized.
5. Curiosity or the thirst for knowledge, which is based on the fear of the unknown (mystery).

The morbid forms of fear are anxiety, anguish, phobias, and collective fears. So, how do we free ourselves from fear, according to Assagioli? We can

---

2. Assagioli, *Transpersonal Development*, 164.

employ *two* types of methods: psychological and spiritual, with the second category being the most effective. Psychological methods include the use of the mind through reason or persuasion; psychoanalysis as an exploration of the unconscious; diversions and substitutions such as sport and physical activities, or humor, or cultivating positive emotions such as courage or hope; psychagogic exercises such as suggestion techniques or affirmations or training of the imagination.

Assagioli asserts that every fear is based on ignorance or error and is overcome—spiritually speaking—at its roots by the light of truth and spiritual realization. Thus:

1. The fear of death is overcome by the spiritual perspective that death does not exist, that when we die our essence continues to exist in a life of greater freedom.
2. The fear of loneliness and isolation (numbers two and three on the former list) is overcome through communion with the Absolute.
3. The fear of failure (an inferiority complex) is overcome by becoming aware of one's latent powers and one's true spiritual nature.
4. Finally, the fear of the unknown and the future is overcome by a) reflecting on the fact that feared ills often fail to materialize, b) that we will not have to endure hardships beyond our ability to cope, and c) growing in wisdom.

Propositions

We can summarize some of the content of this chapter in *fifteen* propositions by way of summary thus:

- Come to know who you are in truth.
- Focus on *what you can control* and change, not on what you can't.
- *Respond* to life's events and experiences with reason rather than *react* with the emotions.
- *Face* your fears rather than *flee* or *fight* them.
- *Perceive*, don't conceive.
- *Abstain* in order to obtain.
- *Face the facts* rather than engage in fantasies.

Formulations on Fear

- *Don't pre-empt* the situation, rather *abide in the present*.
- Realize *you are not your fears*; this is to appreciate the enormous difference between the ego (false I) and the Self (true I).
- *Accept that which is*, wishing to have things happen as they happen rather than attempting to conform the creation to your mind/wishes.
- Remember that *what resists, persists*.
- *Carry out the exercises* adumbrated in this book.
- *Count your blessings* daily.
- Learn to *let go*; practice detachment/disidentification/indifference to indifferent things.
- *Live* your life *from your highest dimension* (Self as Spirit).
- *Fear no evil* and let nothing frighten or anger you, because the inner sanctuary of the Self is inviolable/invincible/impervious.

"We can easily forgive a child who is afraid of the dark; the real tragedy of life is when men are afraid of the light." –Plato

Plato, from Raphael's *School of Athens*

The Nine Faces of Fear

A Prayer and a Petition

May all be free from fear. *Amen.*

For that which is aware of fear is not fearful.

"The present is always lit, because it is the presence of the Absolute, and the light of the Absolute falls on the present. There is nothing to worry about or fear in the present. Past and future are very dark, and that is where the fears are, and it is only fears of some sort which drag individuals to the past or the future. It is much better and more economical for us to avail ourselves of the brilliance and the light and knowledge which are of the present."
–Shantanand Saraswati

3

Fear in Stoic Theory and Therapy

"To him who is afraid, everything rustles." –Sophocles

Epictetus

IN THIS CHAPTER I'D like to engage briefly with Epictetus, whose Stoic quotations have featured throughout, especially in relation to what he teaches about fear.

For centuries, Stoicism was the most influential philosophy in the Graeco-Roman world. Founded by Zeno of Citium in the third century BC who taught from a stoa (a painted porch or colonnade) in Athens, it was to attract into its ranks men as diverse as Epictetus the slave, Seneca the lawyer, and Marcus Aurelius the emperor. In the context of the Ancient classical Greek tradition, philosophy was understood to be a therapy of the soul and the site of spiritual exercises, persuasively argued for by Pierre Hadot in his *What is Ancient Philosophy?* and *Philosophy as a Way of Life*.

It was Stoicism, arguably, that was the preeminent practical philosophy of the time. This older view of philosophy as *praxis*, as a care of the self or cure of the soul, may be traced back to Socrates's maieutic method and more systematically to Plato's understanding of the nature of philosophy itself. Stoicism flourished in Greek and Roman antiquity and is presently enjoying something of a comeback.

A Roman official preserved Epictetus's sermons. Epictetus was lame; his Greek name means "acquired." He was allowed to attend the lectures of

Musonius Rufus, however. He ultimately obtained his (external) freedom. He lived a simple life and taught philosophy in Rome and elsewhere, setting up a school for young men in the Northwestern Greek city of Nicopolis. He was on intimate terms with Hadrian. Like Socrates, he wrote nothing. His *Discourses* and *Enchiridion* were compiled by Flavius Arrianus who attended his lectures. The *Enchiridion* (or *Handbook* or *Manual*) is a condensed selection of Epictetus's sayings, more fully elaborated in the *Discourses*, of which eight books were originally written, with four surviving. In Greek, the *enchiridion* means a little thing for carrying in the hand, thus "handbook." Epictetus's philosophy was to be kept "at hand."

> "Freedom is the prize we are working for: not being a slave to anything—not to compulsion, not to chance events—making fortune meet us on a level playing field." –Seneca

For the Stoic, man's being is one; man is a rational creature; his "guiding principle" is reason, which is a fragment of the divine. The Stoic will highlight the importance of the power of reason and the independence of the will. Through our inner attitude we can attain real freedom. The chief concern of Stoicism is with character and conduct—the sphere of the soul, the highest good (virtue) and conformity with nature (reality). Feelings, such as fear and desire, are not true to man's nature—they are in fact the product/result of false judgements/beliefs. Man is master of his fate; every action is his own choice, and every choice has a consequence.

Mention is made by Epictetus of the life of Rome—the ambitions of high office, the Emperor, the festivals and games, the beggars and the philosophy schools. His practical philosophy takes place against the background of all the vanities and vices of the world. It is philosophy rather than religion which forms the basis for life. His philosophy embodies a wise cheerfulness. He encourages us to play the game of life out, to remain detached and independent, even as we fulfil our social obligations as citizens. Key Stoic terms include:

- Governing Principle (*Hegemonikon*)
- Feelings (*Pathos*)
- Perception (*Aisthesis*)
- Reason (*Logos*)
- Soul/Spirit (*Psyche*)

- Preconception (*Protepseis*)
- Judgements (*Dogmata*)

And the word *phantasia* can be translated as "imagination" or "impression," "appearance," or "presentation." For the Stoics, impressions are not the truth. Stoicism does not offer any consolation for the continuance of the soul. But for the brief moment that man finds himself in this great human gathering—this Olympia of life—his consciousness is cast to play a part upon the stage, and we ought, the Stoics maintain, to play it with as much dignity, depth and detachment as possible (not to become attached to any part in the play).

> "Whoever wants to be free should wish for nothing or avoid nothing that is up to other people." –Epictetus

Freedom is Epictetus's favorite theme, especially freedom from fear. Freedom entails fearlessness. We can be externally free and internally a slave, dominated by psychological masters in the form of disordered desires. Conversely, one could be in literal bondage but internally free of frustration, thus experiencing *apatheia* ('being unaffected') and *ataraxia* ('being undisturbed'). Epictetus's emphasis is on personal well-being rather than politics. Our mind *is* us. Happiness is not conditional on circumstance. If one can flourish in adversity, one can equally fail in prosperity. The difference is in our attitude or mind. Emotional freedom is the heart of Epictetus's message. What is *naturally free* are all those things that are "up to us," in other words, within our power to change and control. Epictetus devotes book 4, chapter 7 of the *Discourses* to "On Freedom from Fear."

> "If man has once entered a philosopher's lecture-room and does not know what his true self is, he deserves to fear." –Epictetus

Man is not his flesh or blood or bones or sinew. He is the faculty that uses and governs them. The mind is his "ruling faculty."

> "No one who is in a state of fear or sorrow or tension is free, but whatsoever is delivered from sorrows or fears or anxieties is at the same time delivered from servitude." –Epictetus

> "We must be afraid of neither poverty nor exile nor imprisonment, of fear itself only should we be afraid." –Epictetus

> "It is not death that a man should fear, but he should fear never beginning to live." –Marcus Aurelius

Freedom is "an independent and unhindered existence."[1] He advises us not to add conceptions to the facts. "No one who is miserable can be free."[2] Indeed, "Call him a slave, though he wears the purple hem."[3] Senators can be slaves, just as slaves can be freemen. No one can compel your will; you give assent or not to feelings. If you adopt the Stoic attitude of being indifferent to externals, then "no man can inspire fear in you any longer."[4] So, how exactly is your inner citadel destroyed? Not by fire or sword, Epictetus contends, but by your *judgements*. We need to enjoy the festival that is life and not be held hostage by fear or anger. The power of assent is the mental faculty that conditions a person's capacity to approve or disapprove of the truth value of impressions (appearances). We forfeit our freedom too easily. Real freedom is inner freedom; it consists in that state of mind that is characterized by being free from frustration and fear.

No negative news can affect you within the region of the will. Your will is free. If you so will it, you're free. No one has authority over you. The 'will' is the power of self-determination and mental disposition. Why do you still fear, Epictetus enquires? What did you learn in the philosopher's school? Keep your imagination in check; don't let it get the better of you. Don't concern yourself with things outside your will. Win inner freedom from fear and the tyrant will cease to exist for you. What makes us free is our judgements (beliefs) about things.

> "How can we call him free when he has not learnt to give up desire and fear?" –Epictetus

Attend to what is in your will/power—on what you can control, and if you do this, "What room is left for anxiety?"

Stoics such as Epictetus were anti negative emotions not positive ones. Indeed, they insist on draining joy to the dregs without delay, as Seneca puts it in his *Epistles*. They want us to favor reason, stay detached from externals and free. Fear, for them, is a form of foolishness. The Stoic technique is to identify the state of mind that is responsible for fear and reform it. Fear

1. Epictetus, *Discourses*, 4.1.
2. Epictetus, *Discourses*, 4.1.
3. Epictetus, *Discourses*, 4.1.
4. Epictetus, *Discourses*, 4.1.

multiplies our problems. If something is going to be bad in the future (and frequently it turns out not to be) then why drag it into the present since this entails suffering twice?

"What it fears lest it suffer, it suffers already through fear." –Seneca

We thus torture ourselves. Fear overdraws misfortune. It is ruinous of our minds that they worry about the future. Such a mind will never be at rest, will never enjoy even a modicum of peace. In being fearful about the future it loses sight of what it might have enjoyed in the present.

"The fear of losing a thing is as bad as regret at having lost it." –Seneca

We thus act like deer; when frightened we flee. Reason must prevail. Stoicism sees in fear a kind of sickness, akin to slavery. We mainly exist in a fever of anxiety. For Stoics such as Epictetus and Seneca, fears are opinions about what is to come. Fear is defeated by dismantling erroneous beliefs about it. Rational scrutiny dissolves fears. One antidote: fix the game in our favor. Favor your own side. Don't borrow trouble. The feared thing might not happen. It may happen in the future but it's not happening right *now*. Unexpected things do happen just as expected things never come to pass.

"Perhaps it will be, perhaps it will not be; meanwhile it is not." –Seneca

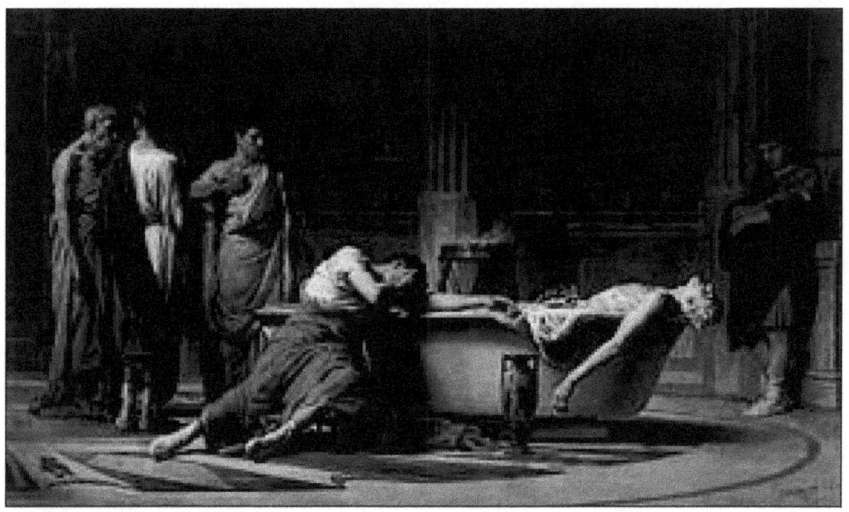

The Death of Seneca by Manuel Domínguez Sánchez (1871).

So, circumscribe your mind and keep it fixed on the present. Furthermore, what if the feared event actually does happen? Maybe it's not so bad after all. Moreover, what we fear is sometimes not great or of long duration. Also: some things we fear turn out to be for the best.

Happiness and freedom begin with a clear understanding of one principle: "Some things are within our control, and some things are not." This is the cardinal Stoic maxim. Learn to distinguish between what you can and can't control. Trying to control or change what is outside your power to do so results in anxiety. We need to always remember that it's not things themselves that trouble us but our beliefs (conceptions/interpretations) about such things. We should be able to say, "You're only an impression—just an appearance—and in no way the real thing" (*neti, neti*). Every situation has two handles, making it supportable or insupportable. Don't fasten onto the negative. Epictetus asks: "Do you wish to live in fear and sorrow?" No-one who "is fearful or sorrowful or disturbed is free."[5] Freedom is self-determination, auto-telic. Horses and houses are not up to us. He puts it to us: "Can anyone make you assent to something untrue?"[6] No. In the domain of assent we are unimpeded, unconstrained. No-one can compel you to desire something you don't want. Epictetus urges us to behave as if we were at a banquet. Take a portion or a plate and pass on. Don't let your appetite run away. If we act like this in all things, one day we shall "dine with the gods."[7]

Let's offer a Stoic laundry list, summarizing the worldly wisdom of Epictetus based on *The Art of Living*:

- Know what you can and can't control/change and focus your attention on the former.
- Learn to distinguish between the appearance of a thing and the reality of a thing, saying 'You're just an impression and by no means what you appear to be.'
- Reign in your desires because they are insatiable ('mercurial rulers') which lead only to disappointment.
- Open your eyes and see things for what they are. Things (and people) are not what they appear to be.

---

5. Epictetus, *Discourses*, 3.24.
6. Epictetus, *Discourses*, 3.22.
7. Epictetus, *The Enchiridion*, 15.

- Things don't hurt or hinder you. Nor do other people. It's your reaction that gives you problems. You can't choose your circumstances, but you can choose how you respond to them.
- Attitude is all.
- Don't add to things (conceptions). "It's not the things that disturb us, but our interpretations of their significance." What frightens you is the way you think about things not the things themselves.
- Practice detachment especially from "clinging thoughts and feelings." Consider your favorite cup. If it breaks, you could still cope, couldn't you?
- Don't play the blame game or depend on the admiration of others. Create your own merit. Be happy with yourself.
- Don't get distracted by trifles. Keep your attention directed at the ship; listen for the call of the captain.
- Accept events as they happen, not as you wish them to happen.
- You're always in control of yourself; your "will" (attitude, mindset) is in your power.
- An obstacle is an opportunity. Endure trials as they will introduce you to your inner resources (strength of spirit).
- Nothing can be taken from you. There is nothing to lose. Things are on loan to you. That is all. Enjoy them as long as the world lets you, like a traveler who takes care of his room at the inn.
- Progress in life results in inner freedom from turmoil and agitation. Stop fretting about the small stuff.
- Figure out what is essential and what is trivial. Stick to your purpose.
- Conform your desires to reality rather than trying to bend reality to suit your desires. You won't succeed. Freedom comes from understanding the limits of your power.
- Don't be swept away by your emotions. Stick to the facts about things.
- Avoid adopting other people's opinions on things, especially negative ones. They can be contagious. Don't let yourself be pulled too much into other people's problems.
- We are like actors in a play so act well the part that has been given you. Whatever role you find yourself in, give a sterling performance.

- As you think, so you will be. Avoid investing conceptions and meanings on events which they simply don't have.
- Happiness can be found only within. "Freedom is the only worthy goal in life."
- Other people don't have the power to hurt you unless you let them. Take a wider view of things. Compose yourself.
- Face the realities of false hopes and disappointments. Don't turn away from the suffering of the world, "from the painful events of life." We walk among good and evil.
- Attach to what is spiritually superior.
- Be a lover of wisdom and a seeker of truth.
- Better to be a good person than a wealthy person. Integrity is everything.
- Learn to accept events, especially death.
- Happiness is won by being your best Self.
- Treasure your mind; cherish your reason.
- You have a choice: concentrate on and lose yourself to externals, or focus on internal work, which is the path to wisdom.
- Locate yourself in the cosmic scheme of things.
- Know that the divine order is intelligent, that life is not random or meaningless but an elegant whole with comprehensible natural laws.

"Our hopes and fears sway us, not events themselves." –Epictetus

- Refrain from personalizing an event, saying "This is my misfortune." Look for the opportunity in the obstacle. There is no such thing as a good or bad event.

"The wise man knows it is fruitless to project hopes and fears on the future. This only leads to forming melodramatic representations in your mind and wasting time." –Epictetus

- Explicitly identify the type of person you want to be.

- Think before you speak. Be mindful with your words. Mindless and frivolous talk has no merit. Don't be a chatterbox.
- Your life is short—you have important things to do.
- Be careful whom you take on as friends. Be in good company, from books to people. Be selective. Be a positive influence on others. Regularly ask yourselves, "How are my thoughts, words and deeds affecting my family and friends?" Are you doing your part for the spiritual progress of humanity? Draw out the best in others by being an exemplar.
- Take care of your body as it promotes wellbeing and health.
- Sex is not a game. Take it seriously. It has enduring emotional consequences.
- If someone criticizes or abuses you, tell yourself (or them), "They don't know all my other faults."
- Comport yourself as if you were a distinguished person, but without puffed up pride.
- Emulate worthy role models.
- Exercise discretion when conversing. There is no need to be glib or the class clown. Avoid obscenities. There is power in being silent.
- Dispassionately discern and decide, prioritizing and preferring enduring satisfaction to immediate gratification.
- Courtesy and good manners have their place.
- Don't be someone you're not. You have your unique vocation.
- Safeguard reason.
- Avoid excess. Observe proper proportion and moderation. Find true measure.
- People spend so much time on outward appearance. What about inner excellence? Care too about your mind, not just your body.
- When someone gets the wrong measure of you, that's their problem. Of course, they do. They can't see you as you see yourself. Mistreatment comes from false impressions. Say, "It seemed so to that person. But that is just his impression."

- Everything has two handles—one by which it may be carried, the other by which it can't. For example, if a friend mistreats you, don't grab the handle of hurt. Do the opposite. Give what you lack. Grasp the handle of love.
- Study clear and critical thinking lest you be hoodwinked. Logic will serve you well.
- Give your assent to what is true, not to what is an interpretation or an impression.
- Wisdom is communicated more through actions than through words. And living (embodied) wisdom is far more important than theoretical principles and propositions.
- Both help and harm come from within yourself. You are the source of everything good or bad for you. Watch out for the direction of your own desires.
- Live your ideals. Put principles into practice. Stop procrastinating. Decide to be extraordinary. Your nobler Self can't wait any longer.
- *Corragio, corragio* (courage, courage): Be brave. Philosophy, which is the art of living a good life, asks us to move into fortitude. Philosophy is intended for everyone. Its purpose is to illuminate the ways in which our souls have been affected/infected by unsound beliefs. The aim is to flourish virtuously. And flourishing depends on Self-sufficiency rather than on fleeting external pleasures.
- Behold the world as it is—through the eyes of a beginner or lover.
- Information and opinion are not the same as transcendent wisdom.
- Look and listen. Notice what's actually happening, not what you think is happening or wish were happening.

"By the steady but patient commitment to removing unsound beliefs from our souls, we become increasingly adept at seeing through our flimsy fears." –Epictetus

- Goodness exists independently of our conception of it. The Good is eternal—it has been there before we began even to exist.
- Examine things as they appear to your own mind, objectively. Take charge of your own thinking and rouse yourself from the daze of

unexamined habit. Be ever watchful. The wise aren't tricked by the way things appear to be.

- View yourself as a citizen of a world-wide community (*cosmopolis*).
- Don't let personal desires or narrow self-interests color your judgement. Objective externals have no bearing on your happiness.
- Books aren't just to be read; they are to make you think and be better.
- Choose your personal associations with care and monitor the thrust of the conversations you have with them.
- Forgive—both yourself and others. Over and over.
- If you start something, finish it. If you say you're going to do something, do it: consistency over what is comfortable and convenient.
- Wean yourself from attachment to others. You are born into essential goodness.
- Understand wrong-doers; pity perpetrators rather than yield to anger.
- Our true purpose is virtue, which leads to enduring happiness. Pursue the good. To be good is to be happy.
- Never lose sight of what's important and what isn't. See clearly; choose wisely. Determine what is of value.
- Because questions are the engines of reason, and reason is such an indispensable instrument, in that it can distinguish error from truth, frame questions sensibly.
- Don't frenetically chase after every sage or fashionable book. "Become your own soul's doctor."
- Stay the course. Practice the attitude of gratitude. Take the long view of life. Give thanks to the Absolute.
- Practice Self-containment.
- Every habit is fed by repeated action. Whenever you are angry, you increase your anger. You have increased a habit and fueled the fire. If you don't want a temper, don't feed the habit. In time, habits weaken and die, to be replaced by wiser responses.
- "Caretake *this* moment. Immerse yourself in its particulars. Respond to *this* person, *this* challenge, *this* deed." Inhabit the present situation. Participate in the *now*. When the doors are shut and your room is

dark, you are not alone. The Absolute is present always. Give your best, so, to the universe without delay.

"If you would enjoy real freedom, you must be the slave of philosophy."
–Epicurus

REBT

I would like now to consider a very practical form of therapy, which was influenced by Epictetus and other Stoics, by way of including a short clinical dimension to the discussion so far, especially as it can be easily applied to feelings of fear.

Rational Emotive Behavior Therapy (REBT), founded a decade before Aaron Beck's cognitive therapy, is a philosophical and empirically based psychotherapy that has helped people who have experienced fears and phobias. Its central thesis is this, and it relates to what we have been saying above: that people have erroneous beliefs about events that can cause psychical disturbance. These beliefs, however, can be dissipated and dissolved. REBT was first expounded in the mid-1950s. REBT was developed by Albert Ellis, an American psychologist, who was inspired by Stoicism, together with Confucius and Buddhism. Ellis himself experienced numerous fears and anxieties such as asking girls on a date, as well as speaking in front of groups of people.

It's both a system and school of thought. The aim is to see or spot the irrationality of our fears (or other emotions) and replace them with facts, so that the story we tell ourselves about our fears and phobias gets shrunk. It involves **d**isputing **i**rrational **b**eliefs (**DIBS**). Of course, there can be **h**ealthy **n**egative **e**motions (**HNE**s), for example, being afraid when confronted with a tiger or polar bear in the wild, and **u**nhealthy **n**egative **e**motions (**UNE**s), when we hold onto our fears so that they encircle everything and become our constant, cajoling companion.

Ellis's proposition is this Epictetan one: that we are rarely emotionally affected by external events but rather by our own thinking about such events. Everything has to do with how the mind interprets such events. To a large extent, we construct our own thinking; some of these schemas will be positive, others maladaptive. They will be highly evaluative and emotional, but also cognitive and behavioral.

As I have written, in detail, about Frankl's school of logotherapy and existential analysis in *Applied Logotherapy: Viktor Frankl's Philosophical Psychology* and in my online Udemy course entitled, "Therapy Technique for Fears, Phobias, Anxiety and OCD," paying particular attention to the logotherapeutic technique of "paradoxical intention," I will confine my comments here to discussing the primary features of REBT instead.

The model of REBT can be summarized as A-B-C-D-E-F.

A—The **A**dversity

B—The developed **B**elief in the person in relation to the adversity

C—The **C**onsequences of that person's beliefs

D—The person's **D**isputes of A, B and C

E—The **E**ffective new belief that develops

F—The **F**eelings of one's self either at or after point C or E

Sometimes, it's shortened to just A-B-C. According to Ellis, it's not an **A** (the **a**dversity or the **a**ctivating agent) that is causing dysfunctional behavior and their **c**onsequences (**C**s) but what the person irrationally **b**elieves (**B**) about the **a**dversity (**A**). A can be an event or thought or feeling and refer to past, present or future. The **B**s (irrational **b**eliefs) are either explicit or implicit philosophical meanings and assumptions.

If a person's **B** (**b**eliefs) about the **A** is fictional or absolutist, then the **C** (emotional **c**onsequence) is likely to be self-destructive and self-defeating. By understanding our interpretations, we can go to **D** (question the reasons for them) then **E** (which reinforces the notion that no evidence exists for any of their psychopathological philosophy). This new perspective/attitude leads to healthier constructs—**F** (new, more positive feelings).

Ellis holds that there are some core cognitive beliefs that hurt or harm us, such as, "I must do well" which, contributes to anxiety and depression, when we don't do well; or "other people really should treat me well," which can often cause rage in us when they don't; or, "I am entitled to live a hassle-free life of pure enjoyment," which can cause anger or avoidance or frustration when reality doesn't let us. At the bottom of such beliefs are demands. We demand success or fair treatment from life, or we engage in catastrophizing or "awfulizing" (viz., mental magnification—elevating thoughts from bad to worse and from worse to a holocaust of horror), or generalizing or employing "shoulds," "musts," "oughts," and "cants" in our speech. We ignore the positive dimension. We believe we can't tolerate adversity, in other words, low frustration tolerance. There are also secondary disturbances, whereby we disturb ourselves about our disturbances and about our inadequate attempts to overcome them (possible because we think about our thinking; we actually think about thinking about our thinking). Of course, thinking, emotions, and action are three interrelated areas of overlap, rather than separate or disparate sets of functioning. An emotion is a type of evaluative thought. Emotions inform thinking and thinking impacts on feelings. Both influence behavior. REBT, thus, proposes a multimodal model.

> "Work on philosophy—like work in architecture in many respects—is really more work on oneself. On one's own conception. On how one sees." –Ludwig Wittgenstein

> "You must change your life." –Rainer Maria Rilke

Of course, insight alone rarely produces change. Continual work on oneself is required, involving actively disputing with one's beliefs and acting against 'natural' tendencies (habit—the mechanical mind), in order to dissolve one's fears or compulsions. The REBT model is helpful but would need to be incorporated into a fuller psycho-spiritual therapeutic modality such as, I would contend, logotherapy. The technique of 'dereflection,' which involves the movement of the senses outward away from sources of anguish, is especially useful. It involved metacognition. The trajectory is from egoic-identifications to the unattached Self.

If we live out our lives just from our ego-selves, then we will fear both our shadow at morning striding to meet us and our shadow at evening rising to greet us. "I will show you fear in a handful of dust," wrote T. S. Eliot in *The Waste Land*. But only the ego is full of fear and foreboding. The Self, however, knows neither memory (past) nor desire (future) as it abides in the space of the silent, fearless Now.

4

The Enneagram: Nine Foundational Fears

"Nothing in life is to be feared, it is only to be understood. Now is the time to understand more, so that we may fear less." –Marie Curie

Introduction

IN THIS FINAL CHAPTER, we explore the Enneagram system, for *three* main reasons:

1. The Enneagram is conceptually congruent with the philosophy adumbrated thus far, as well as being highly practical, which is in keeping with the thrust of the book.
2. The Enneagram makes clear that the nine enneatypes can be viewed as ego-types; behind them is our essence (this distinction has been in the background of this work).
3. Each type is governed by a specific fear, which the Enneagram allows us to adduce.

The Enneagram helps us realize that we are not our personalities, and that we don't have to always react in the same habitual ways. Through the Enneagram, we discover that a change in our sense of selfhood will occur so that we begin to reside less in our (outer) personality manifestations and more in the (inner) witnessing presence. Fixation upon the personality begins to wane and the deeper roots of identity begin to emerge, which is our real freedom. So, in turning to the Enneagram, we shift gear: we move from considering the *universal* aspect of fear to its *unique* features, to *nine* faces of fear, in fact. Different types will do different things with fear: externalize through hoarding, paranoia etc; repress through avoidance which may manifest as surrounding oneself with safety, security, and suspiciousness of strangers; internalize through keep it to oneself which manifests as denial.

Introduction to the Enneagram

The Enneagram is a powerful and persuasive system of personality that illustrates *nine* archetypal human character structures. The word derives from *ennea* meaning "nine" in Greek and *grammas* meaning "figure." It is thus a nine-pointed figure and is uncannily accurate. According to the enneagramatic model, each of us is born with a dominant type represented by number one to nine (not a scale of superiority). It alerts us to health (integration) and neurosis (disintegration). The enneatypology is more akin to Freudian psychoanalysis than the Myers-Briggs (and Singer-Loomis Type Deployment Inventory), which is based on analytical (Jungian) psychology. That said, the Enneagram is an extremely sophisticated, spiritual system. It combines the insights of perennial philosophy with the findings of modern psychology.

Sacred geometry was practiced by the Pythagoreans who were interested in the meaning of numbers. This line of mystical mathematics was passed on through Plato and Plotinus, the latter being the author of the *Enneads*, which spoke of the nine divine qualities of creation.

The Enneagram emerged from a Sufi tradition which may have found its way into Christianity through Pseudo-Dionysius, Evagrius and some Franciscan mystics such as Ramon Llull (a philosopher and tertiary). More recently, in the nineteenth century, it resurfaced through the teachings of the Russian, George Ivanovich Gurdjieff, which were adopted by his student, P. D. Ouspensky. In 1970, Oscar Ichazo (South America) added to the system and in 1990, Claudio Naranjo, MD (Chilean psychiatrist), Ichazo's student, further extended its range by relating it to existential philosophy. Naranjo taught that the Enneagram and the Tarot came out of the same tradition. The Tarot depicts stages on the path of realization, a teaching that was passed on by one of Ichazo's students. In the early 1970s Friar Robert Ochs, SJ (and many other Jesuits), took over the Enneagram for the purposes of spiritual direction and as a model for the work of the Ignatian *Spiritual Exercises*, as well as other luminaries such as Helen Palmer, A. H. Almaas, and Sandra Maitri, all of whom studied with Naranjo. Ochs introduced it to Jerome Wagner, Don Riso and Richard Rohr, amongst others. These are just some of the names of the leading lights. There have been so many models and maps of the psyche and personality typology over time. The Enneagram harmonizes philosophy, psychology, and spirituality. Truly, it is a "mirror of the soul."

Hippocrates, the Greek physician, traced his *four* temperaments (sanguinary, melancholic, choleric, phlegmatic) to various bodily fluids. C. G. Jung postulated the existence of *four* functions of consciousness: thinking, feeling, sensation and judgement and *two* attitude types: introversion and extraversion, thus combining and culminating to produce *eight* possible psychological types (e.g., extravert-thinking etc.). The psychoanalyst, Fritz Riemann, assumed *four* basic fears: the fear of nearness, the fear of distance, the fear of change, and the fear of permanence, which results in *four* types: schizoid, depressive, compulsive, and hysterical. Muslims, influenced by Christian monasticism, set up spiritual brotherhoods reminiscent of the later Franciscans who were possibly influenced by the Sufis, as we alluded to above. So, all the various discoveries, spiritual dynamics and crossovers flowed into the Sufi symbol of the Enneagram which was called the 'face of God,' because they saw in the nine points of energy, which the Enneagram describes, the nine refractions of one divine love. The Enneagram consists of a circle whose circumference is broken up by nine points, numbered clockwise from 1 to 9, as the diagram below depicts.

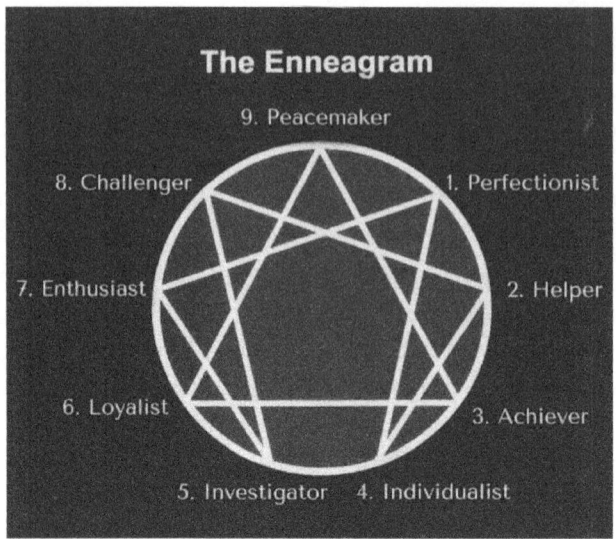

Points 3, 6 and 9 are bound together by an equilateral triangle, while a hexagon of arrows runs through points 1, 4, 2, 8, 5 and 7. The Enneagram came down to us through an oral tradition. Gurdjieff described it as a *perpetuum mobile* and compared it to the 'philosopher's stone.'

The Enneagram is a circle of nine points. One can multiply nine with any number and yet the total of the digits will always be nine. For example, 9 x 2 = 18 and 1 + 8 = 9; 9 x 4 = 36 and 3 + 6 = 9. So, the number nine is seen as the perfect number. Ten is one and zero. *These are nine steps to unity.*

The Enneagram Symbol

The Enneagram symbol has *three* parts that represent *three* divine laws:

1. The circle: a mandala symbol. This refers to wholeness and oneness (God is One). It is the unmanifest source.

2. The triangle: this is in the circle and refers to the Trinity (of Father, Son and Spirit) in Christianity. Hinduism, for its part, talks of Vishnu, Brahma, and Shiva. The universe is a manifestation not of duality but of trinity. Gurdjieff called this phenomenon the "Law of Three."[1] (For example, in terms of physics, on the subatomic scale,

---

1. See Gurdjieff, *In Search of Being*.

atoms are made of protons, electrons and neurons). It's the first manifestation.

3. The hexad: this is the figure tracing the numbers 1-7-5-8-2-4-1 (1÷7) (integration/evolution) and 1-4-2-8-5-7-1 (disintegration/devolution) and refers to the "Law of Seven."

When the three elements are put together (the circle, the triangle and the hexad), you get the Enneagram—a symbol showing the wholeness of a thing (the circle); how its identity is the outcome of the interaction of three forces (the triangle); and how it evolves over time (the hexad)—movement. The Enneagram symbol accounts for human nature in its unity (the circle) and how it is divided (the triangle and hexad).

One way of understanding the Enneagram is to see it as depicting nine lenses through which we perceive the world. Usually, we look *through* rather than *at* our lenses. But with the Enneagram, what's important is not what you're looking *at*, but where you're looking *from*. Human cognition is more telescopic in nature than kaleidoscopic. If you look into a kaleidoscope, you only see the inside of a kaleidoscope. If you look through a telescope you see what is outside the telescope itself.

> "What is *seen through* the perspective, however subjective the perspective may be, is the objective world." –Viktor Frankl

"Seen through" is the literal translation of the Latin word, *perspectum*. Childhood experiences, learning, conditioning, temperament all interact to influence how we see ourselves and the world and how we make sense of our experiences. Our self-understanding is crippled by preconceived patterns of interpretation and indoctrination. Templates are created—paradigms. Such schemas may accurately represent reality or distort it. Schemas are like filters, constructs. We all wear a pair of conceptual glasses. We can either *accommodate* (redraw our maps to align with reality) or *assimilate* (try to fit the world to our mind-maps). The Enneagram shows how we can adjust our lenses, broaden our focus, correct our perceptual (scopic) vision by adding bifocals and trifocals—if you want to see yourself and others more clearly, that is. By so doing, our perspectives enlarge; the Big Picture emerges. From a spiritual point of view, divinity descends and shows itself through *nine* earthly manifestations. Each enneatype is the expression of an egoic perspective; we see through the subjective filter of the ego. The Enneagram is like a prism, designed to help us attune ourselves to (objective) reality. *Essence is all.*

Three Centers, Three Energies, Three Passions

According to the Enneagram system, there are *three* Centers or nuclei: heart, head and gut. Or: *feeling, instinctive* and *thinking* types respectively, which correspond to *three* energies. Heart-people move *towards* you; head-cases (!) move *away*; and gut people (doers) move *against*. To put it another way, the dominant quality of gut people is action while thinking is the dominant quality of the head-types and feeling is the dominant quality of the heart-types—they think that their subjective feelings are in fact objective. It means that the ego has formed around this particular function, be it instinctive, thinking or feeling. The instinctive types are concerned with maintaining resistance to reality; the feeling types with self-image; and the thinking types with anxiety (underneath their ego defenses they carry a lot of fear). No matter what type we are, our personality contains all three components. These three Centers are expressions of the Law of Three, which applies to everything in the universe and humanity.

Furthermore, the dominant passion of the gut-types (Eight, Nine and One) is *anger*; the dominant passion of the heart-types (Two, Three and Four) is *shame*; and the dominant passion of the head-types (Five, Six and Seven) is *anxiety*. But these passions will be modulated, according to type. For example, a One will be ashamed of his/her anger, whereas an Eight won't care about his/her anger. We always remain *true to type*.

This triadic structure is similar to the biological division of the reptilian brain, limbic system (paleo-mammalian) and neocortex. As far back as the fifth century, Plato had offered the image of a winged chariot pulled by horses and guided by a charioteer to describe the interrelationships among the physical center (the chariot), the emotional center (the horses), and the intellectual center (the charioteer). Gurdjieff transported this metaphor into the nineteenth century when he spoke of carriage, horse and driver. Assagioli postulated three realms: the lower unconscious, the middle unconscious and the superconscious, while Viktor Frankl's school of logotherapy set out a tri-dimensional ontology thus: *soma* (body), *psyche* (soul) and *noös* (spirit). Freud had distinguished between conscious, preconscious, unconscious and later between id, ego and superego. Plato had originally proposed a tripartite division of the personality into rational, appetitive and spirited. All 'centers' need to be consulted to circumnavigate the decision-making process and the world.

Earlier, we came across the Eastern trinity, as the Law of Three: *rajas*, *tamas*, and *sattva*. In Sanskrit, the language of the Vedas, energy is described by the word *guna*, as we saw, which means "string" or "rope." *Sattva*, so, is equivalent to neutral energy, *rajas* to positive energy, and *tamas* to negative energy. These three are the cosmic strings of energy (physical, subtle, causal). *Rajas* is active like fire; *tamas* is passive like darkness/ignorance, *sattva* neutralizes and conveys the qualities of light and love, of peace and harmony, of wisdom, stillness, and intelligence.

Moreover, in every new thing arising, *three* forces are at play: (1) affirming, (2) denying, and (3) reconciling/neutralizing. Or: good, bad and indifferent. Or: plus, minus, and equal. The interweaving of these produces a fourth dimension. For example: Active: Father; Passive: Son; Neutral: Spirit. (The fourth dimension would be the world/creation). The order of the forces (direction of development) can change but everything that grows deploys this threefold combination. Other classic examples of Law of Three triads include:

- Seed–Earth: Sun = Sprout
- Flour–Water: Fire = Bread
- Plaintiff–Defendant: Judge = Resolution

Transformation requires the three actions of affirmation, denial and reconciliation, just like the gearbox of a car has forward/drive, reverse and neutral; all three are equally essential. Personality (ego-types) is the mask which covers or camouflages our true Self. To clarify: *Essence is what one is born with*; *personality is what one acquires* through external conditioning. One of the epigrams from "the Work" (i.e., Gurdjieff's system) is: "Behind personality stands essence; behind essence stands Real I, and behind Real I stands God." If essence is natural, personality is artificial. Essence is the "beyond" of personality. We "have" a personality; we "are" spirit. Personality is a variable—changing; Essence is unchanging. Personality is ephemeral, Essence eternal.

To put it another way, one may describe the three types as the destroyer, the converter, and the enquirer. It's the difference between negativity, conviction, and understanding. There are the thinkers, the feelers, and the doers. We may describe these three aspects thus:

- Intellectual: Way of Knowledge: Head
- Emotional: Way of Devotion: Heart
- Physical: Way of Action: Hand

The Fourth Way (P. D. Ouspensky and Gurdjieff) is *moksha* (liberation); it integrates the other three but with detachment. Some (the sages) seem to enter the fourth gate to wisdom directly. Dr Francis Roles (head of the Study Society) met His Holiness Shantananda Saraswati, Shankaracharya of Jyotir Peeth in 1962, where he was asked if the practice in his Advaita tradition was compatible with Ouspensky's teaching of the Fourth Way, to which he replied: "Yes, there couldn't possibly be any difference. He says in his System they take from all the three sources. In the system or 'Way of Action' they purify the heart so as to perform any action and yet be detached from it. the 'Emotional Way' is the 'Way of devotion and Service.' With that an atmosphere is created so as to serve the Absolute and receive His Grace. The third, Intellectual way, is to make Reason work and clarify all the questions met with on the Way, and then if everything is brought together, we hope we are on the 'Way of Understanding,' the Fourth Way."

- Way of the *Fakir*: self-mastery through the physical body involving difficult somatic exercises and postures.
- Way of the *Monk*: self-mastery through controlling the affections in the domain of the heart (faith/devotional dimension).
- Way of the *Yogi*: self-mastery through controlling mental habits and capabilities.

The Nine Types

The Nine types are:

1. The Reformer (or Perfectionist)
2. The Helper
3. The Achiever
4. The Individualist (or Romantic)
5. The Investigator (or Thinker)

6. The Loyalist
7. The Enthusiast
8. The Challenger (or Boss)
9. The Peacemaker (or Mediator)

Overview of the Nine Types

Ones are principled and idealistic, conscientious and ethical, critical and perfectionistic. They are crusaders. They have a problem with repressed anger and impatience. Healthy Ones are heroic, wise, discerning, realistic. They are masters at being correct.

Twos are caring, interpersonal, sincere, warm-hearted, friendly, and generous but also flatterers and people-pleasers. They do things to be needed; they can fail to acknowledge their own needs. They are masters at sensing peoples' needs. Healthy Twos are altruistic.

Threes are success-oriented, self-assured, charming, attractive, ambitious, energetic, competent, competitive. They are status-seekers and driven by personal advancement. They are masters at getting things done. Healthy Threes are authentic, motivating role-models.

Fours are introspective, individualistic, sensitive, reserved, honest. They can withhold. They are masters of drama. Healthy Fours are creative.

Fives are intense, investigators, cerebral, independent, innovative. They are master observers and thinkers. They can become isolated and highly-strung. Healthy Fives are pioneers and visionaries.

Sixes are committed, security conscious, reliable, responsible, hardworking. They can also be anxious, defensive, indecisive, evasive, reactive and rebellious. Sixes are master worriers and loyalists. Healthy Sixes are internally stable and self-confident.

Sevens are productive, busy, optimistic, and spontaneous. They are overextended, playful, exuberant, scattered, resourceful, protective, impulsive. They constantly seek new and exciting experiences which can leave them exhausted and drained. They are master entertainers, storytellers, visionaries, *bon vivants*. Healthy Sevens are joyous and highly accomplished.

Eights are powerful, decisive and dominant, strong and self-assertive. They are power masters who are proud and confrontational. They stand aloof. Healthy Eights are magnanimous and masterful.

Nines are self-effacing and easy-going. They are kind, good-natured, accepting and trusting. They go a long way to keep the peace. They can be passive, obstinate and complacent, minimizing anything upsetting. They are masters of compromise and consensus. At their best, they are all-embracing and affable.

Below is a summary of the positive and negative qualities of each type:

Nine Descriptions[2]

Ones:

Positive

- rational
- idealistic
- orderly
- reliable

Negative

- judgmental
- inflexible
- critical
- controlling

Twos:

Positive

- caring
- loving
- generous
- warm

Negative

- manipulative
- possessive
- overly considerate
- clingy

Threes:

Positive

- ambitious
- efficient
- confident
- practical

Negative

- superficial
- overly competitive
- deceptive
- boastful

---

2. This list is taken from a class, "An Introduction to the Enneagram," taught by Michael Ryan at the Carmelite Centre in Dublin, 2020.

Fours:

Positive

- creative
- expressive
- inquisitive
- introspective

Negative

- self-absorbed
- moody
- depressive
- moralistic

Fives:

Positive

- studious
- unsentimental
- expert
- independent

Negative

- intellectual snobs
- stingy (with their emotions)
- unassertive
- distant

Sixes:

Positive

- loyal
- likeable
- caring
- responsible

Negative

- worrying
- defensive
- suspicious
- blaming

Sevens:

Positive

- outgoing
- curious
- charming
- enthusiastic

Negative

- restless
- escapist
- talkative
- excessive

The Nine Faces of Fear

Eights:

Positive

- dominating
- combative
- direct
- powerful

Negative

- aggressive
- insensitive
- vengeful
- defiant

Nines:

Positive

- easy-going
- patient
- uncomplicated
- optimistic

Negative

- forgetful
- complacent
- disengaged
- inattentive

Nine Values

From the standpoint of the Enneagram, there are nine sets of visions or outlooks:

1. Ones are attracted to goodness—they want to make the world a better place.
2. Twos are attracted to love—they want to make the world a more caring place.
3. Threes are attracted to productivity and competence—they want to make the world a more efficient place.
4. Fours value originality and authenticity—they want to make the world a more beautiful place.
5. Fives value knowledge and wisdom—they want to make the world a more enlightened place.
6. Sixes are attracted to loyalty (fidelity) and consistency—they want to make the world a more safe and secure place.
7. Sevens value joy—they want to make the world a happier place.

8. Eights appreciate power and equity—they want to make the world a more just place.

9. Nines seek peace—they want to make the world a more harmonious place.

Wagner labels Ones as *good* people, Twos as *loving*, Threes as *effective*, Fours as *original*, Fives as *wise*, Sixes as *loyal*, Sevens as *joyful*, Eights as *powerful*, and Nines as *peaceful*. The nine personality styles that we are, are prototypes; we are a mixture of all these preferences. Even if one particular style acts as our core organizing principle, *we are an amalgam of all the types*. Wagner lists the objective principles of each Enneagram Style, with their corresponding virtues, thus:[3]

Nine Personality Paradigms

1. Wholeness
2. Freedom
3. Hope
4. Originality
5. Understanding
6. Faith
7. Work
8. Justice
9. Love

Nine Virtues

1. Serenity
2. Humility
3. Truthfulness
4. Equanimity
5. Non-attachment

---

3. Wagner, *Nine Lenses on the World.*

6. Courage
7. Sobriety
8. Innocence
9. Action

If we lose contact with our core self, our perceptions become solely subjective and distorted, hence, unreliable; our emotions become constricted and contracted and therefore reactive; and our behavior becomes uneconomical (inefficient) and therefore ultimately unsatisfying. This can culminate in nine maladaptive schemas which Wagner names as 'isms' which are forms of idolatry. All idolatry absolutizes that which is relative.

Nine Distortions

1. Perfectionism
2. Situationalism
3. Pragmatism
4. Romanticism
5. Rationalism
6. Fanaticism
7. Hedonism
8. Individualism
9. Quietism

Each enneatype has a core or foundational *fear*, as well as *desire*, that drives them. This fundamental fear is something we defend against with our basic desire. For example, if someone fears being controlled by others, their basic desire would be for freedom (which might deteriorate into escapism, the shadow-side).

The Nine Fears

The gut types (Eight, Nine, and One) are more prone to suffering from *anger*. The heart types (Two, Three, and Four) are more likely to suffer from *shame*. The head types (Five, Six, and Seven) experience *fear* in unique ways. Fives suffer from the fear of being incompetent and insufficient, which drives them to withdraw to compile a competency that they feel will protect them. Sixes suffer from a fear of being without loyalty or support, which leads to them to look for assurance from others. Sevens suffer from a fear of being deprived and depleted, being in a state of lack so they are constantly looking for where to go next to maintain a level of contentment. But it's important to emphasize, that all types suffer from some fear, anger, and shame—the emotional triad of the Enneagram.

Ones: Fear of being bad or corrupt

Twos: Fear of being unloved or unworthy

Threes: Fear of being worthless or without value

Fours: Fear of being without identity or personal significance

Five: Fear of being useless/helpless/incompetent/incapable

Sixes: Fear of being without support/direction or guidance

Sevens: Fear of being deprived or in pain

Eights: Fear of being controlled or harmed by others

Nines: Fear of loss/fragmentation or connection

The Nine Sins

At least seven of the nine enneatypes match the Seven Capital Sins. We can map these directly onto the nine enneatypes thus:

Enneatype	*Capital Sin*
One: The Reformer (Perfectionist):	*Anger*
Two: The Helper	Pride
Three: The Star (Achiever):	*Deceit*
Four: The Romantic (Individualist):	Envy
Five: The Hoarder (Investigator):	Avarice
Six: The Guardian (Loyalist):	Fear
Seven: The Planner (Enthusiast):	Gluttony
Eight: The Bully (Challenger):	Lust

Nine: The Slug (Peacemaker):   Sloth (indolence)

To the existential question, "How should I be?" we can delineate the behavioral style with a cognitive commitment to a particular strategy thus:

The Nine Ways to Be

1. Be correct
2. Be related
3. Be impressive
4. Be sensitive
5. Be retentive
6. Be wary
7. Be pleasing
8. Be pugnacious
9. Be calm

Bernard Lonergan, SJ, the Canadian philosopher and theologian, encourages us to be authentic. For him, authenticity involves obeying the *five* transcendental precepts which we may call 'be-attitudes':[4]

1. Be attentive
2. Be intelligent
3. Be reasonable
4. Be responsible
5. Be loving

These five habits provide us with the basic structure of the healthy psyche. Taken together, the template brings the person to authentic self-transcendence. They are directions to our psyches that we:

1. Open our eyes and ears
2. Ask "why" and "how"
3. Wonder "whether" and "could"
4. Deliberate on "should" and "ought"

4. Lonergan, *Insight*.

5. Seek friendship and love

Our reactions tend to follow the triad of flee-fight-freeze, or dread-desire-deaf. (Anger is traditionally associated with the Eight, Nine and One on the Enneagram; fear with Sixes). There is another triad, that of: head-heart-gut—the three centers. This tripartite perspective on personality bids us to integrate and operate harmoniously. Some will seek authenticity in the world of the head, that is to say, in thinking (Five, Six and Seven); others in the heart, that is to say, in the feelings and emotions (Two, Three and Four); others in gut reactions (Eight, Nine and One). Gut people react instinctively; they are ruled by aggression, but they have little access to their fear and anxiety. They hide behind a façade of self-confidence. Heart people are moved towards others. Their world is one of subjective feelings; their theme, intersubjective relation. The "head-cases" (Fives, Sixes and Sevens) are the thinking types who outwardly appear to be clear, calm and convincing (objective) but inwardly they may be confused and isolated. They are "top heavy." Every type also contains traits of both its neighbors, the "wings." So, Seven's wings are Six and Eight, for example. Taken together, the Enneagram depicts the nine faces of the soul (the point where man and God meet).

Each type has its compulsion. We may define a compulsion as follows: *an autonomic psychic impulse that constricts impulses to be attentive, intelligent, reasonable, responsible and loving.* The names of the nine compulsions are:

The Nine Compulsions[5]

1. Ego-Resent
2. Ego-Flattery
3. Ego-Go
4. Ego-Melancholy
5. Ego-Stinge
6. Ego-Cowardice
7. Ego-Plan
8. Ego-Venge

5. Dunne, *Enneatypes*, 36–68.

The Nine Faces of Fear

9. Ego-Indolent

Naranjo's list is as follows:[6]

1. Perfectionism
2. False Love
3. Deception
4. Dissatisfaction
5. Detachment
6. Accusation
7. Fraudulence
8. Punitiveness
9. Self-Forgetting

The Nine Needs

Heart: Twos need to be needed.

Threes need to succeed.

Fours need to be special.

Head: Fives need to know.

Sixes need security/certainty.

Sevens need to avoid pain.

Gut: Eights need to oppose.

Nines need to avoid.

Ones need to be perfect.

So, in terms of "personality disorders," Ones are *perfectionistic*, Twos are *co-dependent*, Threes are *Type-A* (high-achieving workaholics), Fours are *sensitive*, Fives are *schizoid*, Sixes are *paranoid*, Sevens are *hedonistic*, Eights are *aggressive*, Nines are *passive-aggressive*. It's important to note, however, that *personality (our ego) masquerades as our essential Self.*

---

6. Maitri, *The Spiritual Dimension of the Enneagram.*

There are biases and blind spots. Ones avoid *anger*, Twos avoid their own *needs*, Threes avoid *failure*, Fours avoid *ordinariness*, Fives avoid *feeling empty*, Sixes avoid *feeling dependent*, Sevens avoid *pain and suffering*, Eights avoid manifestations of *weakness*, and Nines avoid *conflict* and disagreement.

Nine Defense Mechanisms[7]

1. Reaction formation
2. Repression
3. Identification
4. Introjection
5. Isolation and compartmentalization
6. Projection
7. Sublimation
8. Denial
9. Narcotization

The Spectrum

Each of the nine types embraces a spectrum which runs from unredeemed/unhealthy/neurotic to redeemed/healthy/mature. Unredeemed persons are trapped in themselves. The redeemed is the saint or the sage—the enlightened one. We're all somewhere in-between. Transcendence is liberation. We're none of these numbers/personalities. They're simply roles we play. The point is to enjoy them without being bound by them. We might outline *three* stages (I owe this insight to Michael Ryan):

1. Spot your own compulsion (as enquiry).
2. See the compulsion in others (as psychology).
3. Realize the same (Self) in both you and others (as philosophy).

---

7. Wagner, *Nine Lenses on the World*.

The Nine Faces of Fear

Nine Noticings

Wagner lists the perceptual acuities of the nine types thus:[8]

1. Ones notice flaws, imperfections, what's wrong.
2. Twos sense who's hurting and who needs what.
3. Threes pick up on what others expect them to be.
4. Fours pick up on disapproval and rejection.
5. Fives will sense any expectations or demands put on them.
6. Sixes will sense danger lurking in the room.
7. Sevens will gravitate towards where the fun and excitement are.
8. Eights will sense who has power in the room.
9. Nines will merge with people, sensing what it's like to be in their skin.

Nine Schemas

Wagner lists the nine "schema avoidance maneuvers," which the nine personality types put and keep in place, thus:[9]

1. Perfection schema
2. Helping schema
3. Achievement schema
4. Troubled, special schema
5. Loner schema
6. Fear schema
7. Pleasure schema
8. Power schema
9. Resignation schema

    The description of the personality types is universal and applies equally to males and females but there is a particular pattern to which we return. We

---

8. Wagner, *Nine Lenses on the World*.
9. Wagner, *Nine Lenses on the World*.

fluctuate among the average, healthy and unhealthy. To repeat: *we have all nine types in us.* The Enneagram helps us to see how trapped we are in our trances, how estranged we have become from our Essence, from what Riso and Hudson call our "Essential nature."[10] Personality is pliant, perspectival; Essence is expansive. *Metanoia* is required—a change or conversion, of mind, heart and behavior. We all possess the potential and the promise for envisioning reality in its entirety. To perceive clearly, we need the perspective of all nine paradigms, which is the God's eye view of everything.

Moreover, Wagner draws our attention to the different ways the nine types communicate:[11]

Nine Speaking Styles

1. Ones instruct and sermonize.
2. Twos flatter, compliment and advise.
3. Threes propagandize/sell themselves and their product.
4. Fours lament.
5. Fives summarize/give epigrammatic replies.
6. Sixes caution and set limits.
7. Sevens embellish and exaggerate.
8. Eights debunk.
9. Nines talk in a monotonous manner.

Outward and Inward Directions

Our ego boundaries fall into two categories: *outward* or *inward*. The directions of ego boundaries in the instinctive triad is out *against* the environment. Each of the instinctive types has a problem with aggression: Eights *act out* their rage, Nines *deny* their anger, and Ones *repress* it. They are concerned with controlling the environment, have issues with aggression and repression, seek freedom and their underlying feeling is *rage*.

For the feeling types, the heart is the source and core of their identity. Twos, Threes and Fours are most concerned with their narcissistic

---

10. See Riso and Hudson, *The Wisdom of the Enneagram*, 17.
11. Wagner, *Nine Lenses on the World*.

wounding and their identity issues as well as problems with hostility and feelings of shame. They are concerned with image and love of false self, have issues with identity and hostility, seek attention and their underlying feeling is *shame*.

The thinking triad is concerned with strategies and beliefs, have issues with insecurity and anxiety and seek security. Their underlying feeling is *fear*. Fives, Sixes and Sevens can't seem to still their minds. Fives retreat from life; Sixes appear to be not afraid of anything and charge into life; and Sevens are afraid of their inner world—of being trapped in emotional pain, grief and anxiety. Sixes, like Sevens, are always anticipating the future. Sixes flee inwards to avoid external threats and outward to avoid internal fears. Sevens flee outwards due to fear of their inner world.

Social Styles

Karen Horney, a follower of Freud, highlighted the *social styles* of each type. Below is another triad:[12]

1. The *Assertives* are ego-oriented; they are the Threes, Sevens and Eights. They demand and get what they want.
2. The *Compliants* are types One, Two and Six (they usually need to be of service to others). These attempt to earn something by placating their superego to get what they want.
3. The *Withdrawns* include Fours, Fives and Nines (preferring their imagination and Inner Space/sanctum). They disengage to get what they want.

Nines, Twos and Sevens have a pretty positive outlook. They deny they have any problems. Ones, Threes and Fives cut off from their feelings to solve problems logically. They are the competent group. Sixes, Fours and Eights are the reactive triad—they need a response from others.

Ego vs. Essence

We are more than our ego-personalities. And this too the Enneagram shows us.

---

12. While Horney did not comment on the Enneagram, some writers have adopted her insights, mainly from Horney, *Neurosis and Human Growth*.

The Enneagram: Nine Foundational Fears

"The spirit is the true self, not the physical figure which can be pointed out by your finger." –Cicero

The Young Cicero Reading by Vincenzo Foppa (1464).

We have fallen asleep as to our true nature. Our essential Self is presence, the ground of Being, Spirit, which takes its dynamic from the soul. If our personality is a particular aspect of our soul, our soul itself is Essence or Spirit. If Spirit is the water, personality is the waves on the water, and soul is the lake or the river. We tend not to experience our Essence which is covered up by our personality. The Enneagram really operates as a bridge between psychology and spirituality. In *The Wisdom of the Enneagram*, Riso and Hudson put it like this: "The core of this sacred psychology is that *our basic type reveals the psychological mechanisms by which we forget our true nature—our Divine Essence.*"[13] Loss of contact with our divine Ground can cause anxiety and fear and assume the form of one of the nine "passions" or "capital sins," we have listed. Even when we make contact with our essential nature, for example, in meditation, we don't lose our personality, but it does become

---

13. Riso and Hudson, *The Wisdom of the Enneagram*, 28.

more transparent. Presence now underlies personality. In meditation, we go backstage; we move from becoming to being. Meditation brings us into the present moment, and this heralds peace. It restores us to our Self, whose secret name is *Aham*—I Am. Just as the body requires sleep to rest, the mind needs to pause between activities, and the spiritual realm needs the inner cleansing that takes place in meditation. These are the *three* aspects of a human being: body (gross), mind (subtle), and spirit (causal).

Fear, one could say, is the result of the inevitable loss of contact with our essence in early childhood, when needs are not met. The basic fears are universal even though each type has its own characteristic basic fear. Each basic fear is a reaction to the universal/ultimate (personality) fear of nothingness. Further, to compensate for this basic fear, a basic desire arises. Desire, one could say, is one way we defend against our fear. The basic desire is what we believe will make us okay; it's the ego agenda. The universal teaching (of the perennial philosophy) suggests that human nature is driven both by fear and desire. The whole of our personality structure can be seen as a flight *from* our Basic Fear and fight *for* our Basic Desire. Our personality emerges out of this dynamic. Our essence, which no traumatic experience can damage or destroy, has been constricted by our personality. The essential 'I' is without personality. To access more of our essence, the movement we should employ is *from identification* to *inner observation*. Also: surrendering our fear of actually being present.

Awareness Leads to Presence

Below are the nice basic desires and their distortions:[14]

The Nine Desires

1. The desire to have integrity (deteriorates into critical perfectionism)
2. The desire to be loved (deteriorates into the need to be needed)
3. The desire to be valuable (deteriorates into striving after success)
4. The desire to be oneself (deteriorates into self-indulgence)
5. The desire to be competent (deteriorates into useless specialization)
6. The desire to be secure (deteriorates into an attachment to beliefs)

14. Riso and Hudson, *The Wisdom of the Enneagram*, 33.

The Enneagram: Nine Foundational Fears

7. The desire to be happy (deteriorates into frenetic escapism)
8. The desire to protect oneself (deteriorates into constant fighting)
9. The desire to be at peace (deteriorates into stubborn neglectfulness)

Riso and Hudson list nine invitations to the nine types based on the strengths symbolized by them:[15]

Nine Invitations

1. To live for a higher purpose
2. To nurture yourself and others
3. To develop yourself for others
4. To let go of the past
5. To observe yourself without judgement
6. To have faith in yourself and trust in the primary goodness of creation
7. To celebrate life joyously and share your happiness
8. To stand up for yourself and speak out for what you believe
9. To bring peace and healing to the world

Two Lenses: Wings and Instinctual Variants

The Enneagram is precise and can pinpoint particular issues for us. Each type has *two* "Wings" and *three* "Instinctual Variants." You will have a type on each side of you which is your Wing. There are, therefore, eighteen wing subtypes. The Instinctual Variants indicate which of our *three* basic instincts have been most distorted in childhood. The three instincts are:

1. Self-Preservative
2. Social
3. Sexual

So, a Seven could be a Self-Preservation Seven or a Social Seven or a Sexual Seven. Altogether, then, there are *six* variations for each type, totaling

---

15. Riso and Hudson, *The Wisdom of the Enneagram*, 42.

fifty-four major variations in the entire Enneagram. The Self-Preservative types are preoccupied with acquiring and maintaining physical comfort; they are concerned with food, clothes, money, housing, physical health. The Social types want to be approved and socialize to have this need met. They yearn to be accepted, appreciated and needed. They are concerned with participating in activities be it family or group or community ones. They are aware of power and social structures. The Sexual types are embroiled in a constant search for connection—not just sexual experiences but anything that promises a rush or fix. They can suss out the most interesting people in a room in a second. But they have difficulties pursuing their own projects as they are always looking outside themselves for someone to complete them.

Levels of Development

We alluded to this briefly above. Each type has *three* main ranges: healthy (high functioning), average ("normal"), unhealthy (dysfunctional). These levels offer a way of seeing our degree of identification with our personality structures. Each level represents an increasing layer of fear and defense. The levels are functions of freedom and awareness. Wake-up calls come when we become more identified with our ego. Riso and Hudson's list is below:[16]

Nine Wake-Up Calls

Ones: Feeling the need to fix everything themselves

Twos: Believing they have to go out to others to win them over

Threes: Beginning to drive themselves for status and attention

Fours: Holding onto intense feelings deriving from their imagination

Fives: Withdrawing from reality into the mental world

Sixes: Becoming dependent on something outside the self for validation and guidance

Sevens: Feeling that something better is available elsewhere

Eights: Feeling they must struggle to make things happen

Nines: Outwardly accommodating themselves to others

---

16. Riso and Hudson, *The Wisdom of the Enneagram*, 80.

Furthermore, each type can manipulate others (the social role), by:

1. Correcting others
2. Creating dependencies on them
3. Charming others
4. Being temperamental
5. Staying preoccupied and emotionally detached
6. Complaining
7. Distracting others and demanding
8. Dominating others
9. Being passive-aggressive

Should the fear become great, each type will engage in *projection*. For example, the Seven who fears that they will be trapped in pain, will themselves cause pain to others. The Two who fears they are unloved will make others feel unloved, etc. Instead of obeying the Golden Rule of "doing unto others as you would have them do unto you," the fearful Nine will "do unto others what they most fear having done unto them." In short, they inflict their Basic Fear on others. Riso and Hudson label this the *Red Flag Fear*—it signals a crisis. Their list is below:[17]

Red Flag Fears

- Ones fear that their ideals are wrong.
- Twos fear that they are driving friends away.
- Threes fear that they are failing, and their claims are fraudulent.
- Fours fear that they are ruining their lives and wasting their time.
- Fives fear that they are never going to find a place in the world.
- Sixes fear that their actions have harmed their security.
- Sevens fear that their activities are hurting or bringing them unhappiness.
- Eights fear that others are turning against them and will retaliate.

---

17. Riso and Hudson, *The Wisdom of the Enneagram*, 84.

- Nines fear that they will be forced by reality to have to deal with their problems.

The Level of Liberation

In the healthy range, the ego identity is in place. However, freedom/liberation/redemption/enlightenment happens to the extent that we no longer identify with the ego. The Basic Fears must be worked through, just as the Basic Desires must be acted on rightly.

Two Directions

The Directions of Integration and Disintegration help us to recognize whether we are *progressing* or *regressing* in our development. If you look at the Enneagram, you will see that each number around the circle has two inner lines attached to it. Eight, for example, has one line to Two and another to Five. Nine has one line to Three and another to Six, etc. One line represents the Direction of Integration, which is the line of natural development toward wholeness, while the other line represents the Direction of Disintegration, which shows what behaviors we manifest when pushed to the limit.

- Direction of Integration: Progression
- Direction of Disintegration: Regression

They move in reverse order. The Enneagram can predict what healthy or unhealthy patterns of behavior will emerge if each type continues to deteriorate in terms of defenses and identifications or ameliorate in terms of being less identified and less defensive. The Direction of Disintegration, which is unconscious and compulsive, occurs when we are in a period of increased stress or anxiety. The psychological danger here is acting out (pathological behavior). Riso and Hudson highlight the directions thus:[18]

The Direction of Disintegration (with reversal)

1. Methodical Ones suddenly become moody and irrational at Four.
2. Needy Twos suddenly become aggressive and dominating at Eight.

18. Riso and Hudson, *The Wisdom of the Enneagram*, 89.

The Enneagram: Nine Foundational Fears

3. Driven Threes suddenly become disengaged and apathetic at Nine.
4. Aloof Fours suddenly become overinvolved and clinging at Two.
5. Detached Fives suddenly become hyperactive and scattered at Seven.
6. Dutiful Sixes suddenly become competitive and arrogant at Three.
7. Scattered Sevens suddenly become perfectionistic and critical at One.
8. Self-confident Eights suddenly become secretive and fearful at Five.
9. Complacent Nines suddenly become anxious and worried at Six.

We can state a psychological principle, thus: *whatever a type represses, returns (is acted out) under pressure in a way indicated by the type's Direction of Disintegration.* The Direction of Integration is therefore the antidote. Riso and Hudson on the Direction of Integration:[19]

The Direction of Integration

1. Angry, critical Ones become more joyful like healthy Sevens.
2. Prideful, self-deceptive Twos become more emotionally aware like healthy Fours.
3. Vain, deceitful Threes become more committed to others like healthy Sixes.
4. Envious, emotionally turbulent Fours become more principled like healthy Ones.
5. Avaricious, detached Fives become more decisive like healthy Eights.
6. Fearful, pessimistic Sixes become more optimistic like healthy Nines.
7. Gluttonous, scattered Sevens become more profound like healthy Fives.
8. Lustful, controlling Eights become more caring like healthy Twos.
9. Slothful, self-neglecting Nines become more energetic like healthy Threes.

A key point: *the personality cannot solve the problems of the personality.* All the personality can do, until the essence is made more manifest, is to try to not get up to its little old tricks. We need to let go of fears and

---

19. Riso and Hudson, *The Wisdom of the Enneagram*, 92.

defenses. These are blockages and covers to our essential nature shining through. When the personality is fear-based, the Self, which is our birthright, is occluded. All plants need to shed dead leaves to grow.

Exercise: read through the detailed descriptions of the nine types below and see if you can detect your and/or your friends' type. You can always do a test to confirm it. I recommend the Riso-Hudson Enneagram Type Indicator (RHETI, version 2.5), which is a scientifically validated, forced-choice personality inventory with 144 paired statements and which takes about forty minutes to complete, available from The Enneagram Institute.

A Detailed Description of the Nine Types

Ones

Ones are idealists, reformers, crusaders, organizers, moralists. They are principled, purposeful, punctual, practical and perfectionistic. The Basic Fear of the One is of being defective in some way. Their Basic Desire is to be good and have integrity. Ones are self-controlled, compulsively neat, honest, dependable, fastidious, emotionally reserved, methodical and responsible. They are a body-based type. They have high standards and tend to see the world in shades of black and white. They are critical, idealistic and intolerant of imperfections. They take life (too) seriously. Ones are deaf to inner desires/experiences, so they fixate on *correctness*, on how things "should" be, are overly critical. Their love relationships are filtered by a screen of "shoulds." They are righteous and *resentful* when things don't go according to plan. When they let go of anger, they can be serene. They are demanding, critical, often dominant in a relationship or conversation but they observe etiquette, so are never overtly rude. They scold and come across as superior, haughty, self-satisfied. They are disciplined, rule-bound, upright, neat. They overcontrol their feelings and smile through their (many) irritations. Beneath their positive persona lurks anger. They seem to listen but are often deaf; usually they are preparing a response or thinking about something else altogether. Some Ones can fixate on having immaculate homes; they can be very anxious. They seek to tell everyone where to be and what to do. They tend to conceal their feelings unless unrequited love occurs in which case their jealousy becomes intense. They can be very self-righteous then flip into being self-critical; they can move from self-satisfied to self-annoyed. When they can't control their environment, they can suddenly discharge intense anger.

The Enneagram: Nine Foundational Fears

Ones tend to be model children, 'clean' (as in anally retentive), idealistic, moralistic, frustrated and disappointed by their own imperfections, dutiful, responsible, serious, compulsive, aware of their responsibilities. Anger is the root sin (meaning separation from the Source and what it leaves in its wake) of the One—they are angry at themselves. They can be full of repressed rage. They are ashamed of their anger. They cannot permit their aggression. It gets dumped in the unconscious. Like steam kettles, their rancor simmers. Their workaholism is an offshoot of this because they work hard to be seen to be good and therefore not bad, angry children. They are under tremendous pressure to do and be good. Their need for perfection means that when they think they have found Mr. or Mrs. Right, fissures soon appear as their loved object can never be the perfect person on the pedestal which the Ones demand.

Unredeemed Ones may lead double lives. They behave blamelessly but their shadow side shows and frequently, as has been the case with "conservative evangelicals," their repressed sexuality can become promiscuous and result in social scandal for themselves and their families. Unhealthy/unredeemed Ones are hypocrites. This means that the opposite, which Rohr calls "the fruit of the spirit" is the reverse of the root sin, so in healthy/redeemed Ones it will be cheerful tranquillity. Ones are nature lovers—rational, balanced, just, good teachers, even if they are very black and white. Rohr says that all Ones live close to the edge of self-righteousness. They also incline to procrastination, especially in decision-making.

Ones are prophets; Riso calls them "reformers."[20] Rohr observes: "ONEs are born Pharisees!"[21] They are likeable so long as they don't take themselves too seriously. Their huge energy is about working for and wanting all or nothing. Ones need to play more, to loosen their rigidity. If they dismantle their judgementalism and resentment, compassion becomes possible. Rohr writes: 'They can learn cheerful *joie de vivre*, if they go to school with the light-hearted SEVENs.'[22]

Ones' basic fear is being bad, corrupt. Their basic desire is to be good, virtuous—to have integrity. They are hyper-responsible. Social Ones are teachers and advocates. Sexual Ones yearn for a flawless relationship with an idealized partner. They fear their ideals may be wrong. They fear criticism. Ones fear abandonment, disloyalty and loneliness. They fear others

---

20. Riso and Hudson, *The Wisdom of the Enneagram*, 44.
21. Rohr, *Discovering the Enneagram*, 44.
22. Rohr, *Discovering the Enneagram*, 48.

will become indifferent to their principles. They fear their ideals may turn out to be wrong. They can get angry at themselves for failing to live up to their ideas, for which they experience guilt. Their potential pathology is obsessive-compulsive disorder—rigid, inflexible positions, self-righteousness, rage, intolerance, obsessive-compulsive behavior, and masochistic self-punishment. Ones flatter because they need to be loved.

Animals associated with (unredeemed) Ones: the Terrier—lots of bark, snappy; the Bee—industrious, sting; the Alsatian—keen on the scent of the bad person. Russia is the symbolic nation of the Ones. Rohr thinks Switzerland may be too with its clocks and cleanliness![23] The color of One is silver—cool and clear.

Probable Ones include: Confucius, Plato, Henry David Thoreau, Noam Chomsky, C. S. Lewis, Mahatma Gandhi, Karl Barth, Nelson Mandela, G. B. Shaw, St. Ignatius of Loyola, John Calvin, and Richard Rohr (of Enneagram fame).

Twos

The Two is the helper, the host, the enabler. The Basic Fear of the Two is being unwanted and unloved. Their Basic Desire is to feel loved. Twos are a feeling-based type. They are full of somatic energy. They discharge their anxiety through talking. They can help to bring out potential in others. They seek approval and want to be liked. They are emotional sponges. They are caring and popular; they are sympathetic and nice. They are also naïve and dependent and proud, thinking they're indispensable. They need to be approved and appreciated. Twos are in thrall to the image. They possess a determination to have an impact on others. This is more to do with being starved of love than pride, though they come across as self-inflated. They experience desire more than dread. They see themselves as having many goals especially in the affective sphere. They don't like imperfection. They can be very generous. They can manipulate the emotions of others. They seductively bait others to capture them. They do show a spontaneous sympathy for the needy. They are relatively quick to throw a tantrum and behave histrionically. They may promise friendship but seldom deliver on it. They adjust their mood to suit the person they're presently with even if they worry about being seen as chameleons.

---

23. Rohr, *Discovering the Enneagram*, 43.

The Enneagram: Nine Foundational Fears

Twos are dominant. They don't like rules. They are rebellious but indirectly so; they are sly, cunning. They come across as independent but still need love. They hanker after pleasure. They don't tolerate tedious routine easily or discipline. Even though they are dominant, they are seldom leaders themselves. They manipulate for gain. They are perceived as free, but they just want to do what they please. They can crave affection. Socially, their acquaintances are seen as friends. They are sexually pushy. They flatter, can be very sweet then aggressive in quick succession. They can act compliantly then become disobedient the next minute. They can project a warm heart (playful, lively) or disdainful persona to those who ignore them. They display an apparent generosity to seduce others, suppressing their real feelings; they can feign affection. They like their mood to be matched. Many Twos have experienced a frustration in love especially in childhood, which they carry with them. They indulge in fickle commitments. They believe solitude is the enemy and that relationships are the source of life. They mistake erotic pleasure for love. Friends and lovers tend to pull away sensing a superficial commitment. They excel at making connections. Twos pour on the charm, then feel frustrated and hurt when this strategy doesn't succeed. Sometimes they won't even be able to distinguish feigned and authentic feelings in themselves. Twos needs a Helper/Mentor figure, whom they will ultimately reject. Their psychological defense is repression (viz., they avoid their own needs and feelings to maintain the self-image of being helpers). They can convert/sometime their repressed feelings into physical symptoms.

Twos are people-pleasers, special friends, caretakers. Their basic fear is the fear of being unloved and unwanted. Their basic desire is to feel loved. They obey their superego demand to sacrifice themselves for others. But by putting other people first, Twos become secretly angry and resentful. They think that by sacrificing themselves they will receive love (especially from the family). They repress their own needs. Healthy Twos are Good Samaritans, outgoing, personable, high-handed. The social Two is everybody's friend. They fear being left out or overlooked. Unhealthy Twos are highly patronizing. Sexual Twos yearn for intimacy. They fear they won't be desirable to the other, so they pursue love and fall prey to fears that others won't spend time with them. They then become increasingly possessive and jealous. They need to be needed. They fear they will drive others away. They can engulf the other person. Pride is the capital sin of the Two, which expresses itself as a form of flattery. Twos feel they haven't been loved enough. Theirs is a disguised neediness. They are rescuers; they collect needy people. They frequently sabotage their own relationships, over-extending themselves. Their potential pathology is hysterical personality disorder—self-deception, delusional entitlement, manipulation, obsessive love, repressed aggression, emotional somatization. Their deepest fear is of being worthless—that nobody will want them in the end.

Italy is the symbolic country of Twos with the ubiquitous presence of the *mamma* who rules and appears loving to all and sundry. The symbolic animal of a Two is the cat or Collie: fickle, affectionate then disdainful. Probable Twos include Mother Teresa, Desmond Tutu, and Pope John XXIII.

Threes

The Three is the motivator, role-model, and achiever. The Three's Basic Fear is not having value outside their achievements. Their Basic Desire is to feel worthwhile, desirable, and accepted. Threes radiate ease and assurance. The Three is the central type of the heart group (which includes Twos and Fours). However, Threes have great difficulty in perceiving their own feelings. As children they tended to be praised and rewarded when they showed themselves to be successful. Indeed, they draw their energy from being successful. Threes are careerists, status-seekers, competitive achievers. They are want-to-be winners. They are optimistic, upbeat, productive, intelligent and physically attractive. They are self-assured. They do everything to illicit praise. They are even more dependent than Twos on the response of others. Threes are capitalists. America is the symbolic country of Threes. Threes admire winners and scorn losers. Their defense mechanism is identification. They become completely involved with projects; they are reluctant to accept criticism. In terms of avoidance strategies, Threes avoid failure. Failing is the Three's major fear. Unredeemed Threes avoid, fear and hate defeat and losing. Threes overestimate themselves. Deceit (untruth) is their root sin. The lie is their truth. Unredeemed Threes don't like depth. They take the image to be the reality. They appear self-confident. They get caught up in vanity. Externals become more important than essentials. Redeemed Threes are truthful, honest, direct.

The symbolic animal of a Three is the chameleon (Threes are clever at adapting themselves to their company), the peacock (Threes present themselves well—they strut their stuff), and the eagle (symbol of power and endurance).

The Three is called to hope. They are invited not to let their feelings atrophy; also, to pay attention to their own depth which is difficult as Threes are always pursuing some project. They need to learn to be alone, to be silent and secluded. They yearn for praise and recognition, but also for love. They despise sickness and fear old age. But Threes need to stand still and not continuously chase new successes and applause. Indeed, Threes measure success by applause.

Threes are stars, crave affirmation and admiration; they are motivated by accomplishment. They are hyperactive, efficient and quick. They are always selling something. They are industrious like beavers. Threes are pragmatic, driven, image conscious. They fear being worthless. They yearn to feel accepted, desirable. They are usually well liked. Often, they have a deep emotional bond to their mother. They sometimes don't know why they are pursuing a certain career path; usually it is to make mother proud.

Healthy Threes are vivacious and outgoing, friendly and generous. They work hard as, for Threes, security and stability come from work, money and material well-being. They are very focused on their careers.

Social Threes are status seekers. Sexual Threes are narcissists. They want to be 'the catch.' They are seductive, working out at the gym to present the perfect body. Their fear is that they will not be able to maintain the projection of the glittering, glamorous image they are so intent on displaying. Unconscious fear of their own desirability sometimes means they will reject people they care deeply about.

Threes fear they will be overshadowed by the accomplishments of others. They fear their efforts won't bring them the attention they desire. So, they will drive themselves even more. They fear losing the positive regard of others. They must always shine, be the best, the Golden Boy/Girl. They believe that their ego is their real self. They can become achievement machines, joyless. Their narcissistic neediness is at the heart of their activities and their quest for superiority. They package themselves as a commodity. They fear failing and feeling empty and depressed.

They fear real intimacy and tend to keep people at a safe distance. They have grandiose expectations. Their potential pathology is narcissistic personality disorder. Threes are self-promoters, propagandists and soloists. Their saving grace (it is all of ours) is that there is no emptiness to the essential self. Healthy Threes are outgoing and generous like Sevens. They are task oriented. The danger is workaholism.

Probable Threes include Christian Bale, O. J. Simpson, Elvis Presley, Christopher Reeve, and Sharon Stone.

Fours

The Four is the individualist, the artist, the romantic, the aesthete, the melancholic. He is the sensitive, withdrawn type—expressive, dramatic, temperamental, self-absorbed. The Four's Basic Fear is having no identity, no personal significance. Their Basic Desire is to find themselves, to create an identity out of their inner experience. Fours tend to endure suffering with quiet strength. Fours are unsure about themselves—their personalities/ego-structures. Even though they are socially awkward, Fours don't want to be alone. They hide from the world. They have a negative self-image and chronically low self-esteem. They compensate for this by constructing a fantasy self. Their big challenge is to let go of feelings from the past as they tend to nurse wounds and fixate on negative feelings. Fours feel they aren't like their parents. Many fantasize that they were mistakenly switched at birth. They identify in the family system with the role of the lost child. They can idealize others who are seen as the source of all goodness.

Healthy Fours combine creativity with ambition and desire self-improvement/advancement. They are perceptive and introspective. The self-preservative Four is a sensualist and materialistic; some are susceptible to alcoholism and drug abuse. Social Fours are outsiders, seeing themselves as unlike everyone else. Unhealthy Fours fear rejection. Sexual Fours experience and express intense longing, infatuation, and the need to be rescued. Envy is their capital sin. Their adage is "misery loves company," so they create rivalries and competitions. Their problem is this: if their identity is based on their feelings and feelings are always changing, then their identity is always changing, and so Fours fear it will disappear. They engage in self-defeating acts. Fours fear that their feelings will not sustain them, so they use their imaginations and fantasies to intensify their feelings. They fear others will not appreciate them, so they play hard to get and self-sabotage. Fours fear that life's demands will force them to give up their dreams and so they despair. Frequently, they fear they are wasting their lives.

Fours want to be special and be treated differently than other people. They create for themselves a negative identity: 'No one understands me' is their catch cry. Envy and negative comparisons develop which take them away from their essential selves and from reality. Fours are moody, hypersensitive and touchy to even minor events and perceived criticism. They become resentful, uncooperative and cripplingly self-conscious. Fours become so focused on their fragile feelings that they feel justified in demanding attention and support for all their emotional needs. They talk in detail about their feelings, problems and issues with life and other people. They are never to blame. It's always somebody else's fault. They dwell on unpleasant moods and withdraw from others to protect themselves. They are temperamental and actually attached to having problems. They sulk and succeed only in driving people away with their storms and silences. Their potential pathology is severe depression or avoidant or narcissistic personality disorder—alienation form self and others, extreme emotional volatility, unstable relationships, outbursts of rage and hostility, long term depression and hopelessness, episodic self-sabotage, and obsessions with morbidity and self-hatred. Fours, above all others, need to remember that feelings aren't facts, that emotional volatility is not real sensitivity. They need to be aware that they can't use others as emotional dumping grounds. Healthy Fours are highly intuitive, creative, and have a subtle sense of humor. Like all types, they need to transform their personality into essence.

Fours are sensitive, artistic, eccentric, vital, energetic. Their life-question is: 'what do you think of me?' Their life is shaped by longing. They feel they have endured a great loss in childhood, as they search for role models and identity. Unredeemed Fours will direct their anger against themselves; what is forbidden will attract them. They are melancholic. Possessions bring little happiness to them. Longing is far more important for the Four than having. Fours find it hard to live in the present. They struggle to be authentic. Sublimation is their defense mechanism—feelings, in other words, are not expressed directly. Fours live in fear that someone else could be more interesting or attractive to their partner. They avoid what is ordinary. They are pig-headed, moody, snobbish. Sweet sadness is their pitfall. Depression surrounds them like a fog. They are 'tragic romantics,' in Helen Palmer's words—vulnerable. They have an affinity with death. Partners of Fours are subjected to the hot-and-cold treatment, now seduction, then rejection. Dramatic scenes are commonplace. Fours smile through tears. Their task is to develop realism and reachable goals.

The Four's symbolic animal is the mourning dove, with its cooing and complaining, with its longing lament. France is their symbolic country (the desire to be special). Probable Fours include Rainer Maria Rilke, Marlon Brando, Marilyn Monroe, James Dean, Edgar Allen Poe, Sylvia Plath, Anne Rice, Johnny Depp, Rumi, and Thomas Merton.

Fives

The Five is the thinker, the innovator, the investigator, the observer, the expert. They think before they act. Their Basic Fear is being helpless, useless, ill-equipped and overwhelmed. Watchful separateness sums up the Five. Their Basic Desire is to be capable and competent. Fives are head people (together with Sixes and Sevens). They are cerebral, perceptive, secretive, intense and isolated. They want to understand how everything in the world works. They need to learn, to take in information. They pursue knowledge relentlessly. Fives fear that they don't have the ability to do things as well as others. They spend inordinate amounts of time observing, contemplating, synthesizing. Their attention is drawn to the unusual, to the overlooked. History is full of famous Fives. The focus of the Five is intense, especially in relation to their minds.

They often report that they didn't feel safe in their families as children, that they felt overwhelmed. They are stuck at the separation stage of childhood. Fives frequently flee from their emotional needs into what is objective. They spend long periods of time on their own. What Fives most want is an unobtrusive life.

Healthy Fives are curious, perceptive, creative, detached, analytic, organized, independent, separate. Unhealthy Fives hoard. Self-preservative Fives are friendly and talkative. Social fives are specialists, academics, scientific. Unhealthy Fives can be controversial, provocative. Sexual Fives are detached.

Fives fear their skills aren't sufficient, that they need to master more knowledge, prepare themselves even better. Fives fear that the needs of others will distract them from their projects, so they shut others out and self-isolate. Fives fear that others will threaten their niche and their sense of security, so they tend to fend people off. Unredeemed/unhealthy Fives fear that they are incapable of finding a place in the world. Because they are so 'heady,' they engage more in mental commentary than with their experiences. They turn experiences into concepts. Fives need to reconnect with the world and with their bodies, lest they become disembodied minds, a Cartesian *cogito*.

Fives mainly relate to others by being an expert. Due to their basic fear of being powerless, they want to feel more confident by becoming a know-all. Their capital sin is avarice—they hoard resources, even though they are the least materialistic of all the types and need few creature comforts. Fives feel that there is not much of them to go around and so they experience emotional depletion; others exhaust them. They can feel crowded and overwhelmed by the expectations of others, engulfed.

The Enneagram: Nine Foundational Fears

They are always preparing for action but never quite getting there. They are paralyzed by their superego feeding them the message that they're only good if they have mastered something completely. They are independent, idiosyncratic loners who can become misfits and misanthropes. They feel their isolation is inevitable. They shun those who seek to help them. They get through life by not asking much of it. They can become absent-minded and vacant. Paradoxically, Fives think a lot about the things they find most frightening. Putting this another way, Fives seek to control their fear by focusing their thoughts on the frightening thing itself, not on their feelings about it. Fives are prone to feelings of apathy, cynicism and meaninglessness. They retreat to the sanctuary of their thoughts/minds. Their potential pathology is schizoid or avoidant personality disorder, the symptoms of which include increasing tendency to self-isolate, physical neglect, chronic insomnia, eccentricity, hostile to help, hallucinations and suicidal ideation. Unredeemed Fives are schizoid, autistic.

Fives can have tremendous insights and understandings; they are very observant (Rohr says their "eyes are like vacuum cleaners!"), always curious, open-minded, inventive, endlessly amused or horrified by the play of life. Fives possess an inner clarity that brings nonattachment. They are receptive, good listeners and researchers. They experience a kind of inner emptiness. They collect thoughts but also silence and like their space. Fives are introverts, calm, objective, hating fuss. They are monks and hermits, bookworms and librarians. They avoid attracting attention to themselves. They protect their private sphere. For Fives, knowledge is power. They want to be informed by everything. They are fascinated by intellectual systems; they like to travel even though emotional withdrawal is their basic defense mechanism. Unredeemed Fives fear concrete commitment. They want to see but not be seen. Their other defense mechanism is compartmentalization. They divide their lives into discrete units, segments, departments. The cardinal sin of the Five is avarice, greed. They are not givers. They are stingy, misers. Their greatest gift is to be good advisors and listeners. Fives have to 'cut loose,' let themselves go. Fives fear doing something that is unreasonable. They are on guard. Fives are attracted to truth.

Their symbolic animals are the owl with his immobile eyes, the fox (loner), and the hamster with its greed and passion for collecting. Probable Fives include Albert Einstein, Agatha Christie, Friedrich Nietzsche, Jean-Paul Sartre, and James Joyce.

The Nine Faces of Fear

Sixes

Sixes are loyalists, guardians, doubters, stalwarts, traditionalists. They are committed, conscientious, security-conscious, suspicious, anxious, responsible, reliable, engaging. The root "sin" (distorted emotion) of Six is fear. Their Basic Fear is of having no support or guidance, of being unable to survive on their own. Their Basic Desire is to find such security and support. Sixes need certainty. They are cooperative team-builders. They are warm-hearted and witty.

According to some Enneagram experts, Six is by far the most frequently encountered enneatype. Sixes are fearful and mistrustful, and full of self-doubt. They are a mass of contradictions: emotionally dependent on others yet they don't reveal too much of themselves, obedient yet disobedient, fearful of aggression yet sometimes highly aggressive themselves. They report that they had violent or cold parents. Sixes don't trust easily. The energy of Sixes can produce the Nazi type whose truth is totalitarian—the words of the Führer having the power of law. They can be self-righteous and dogmatic, despotic even. They are often overcome by a paralyzing fear of failure and in many cases can't complete their studies. If Threes are winners, Sixes are losers. This taking pleasure in losing is masochistic. They have a hard time in accepting praise. Sixes are cautious, careful, hesitant. They disguise the fact that it is fear that is fueling them by compensating for it through seeming carelessness or playing the hard man. They strive for security and show a marked tendency to fundamentalism. Sixes search out hierarchies and authority, such as the police force or army or Church. They like a clear command structure and pecking order. Many lawyers and criminals too are Sixes. They are devil's advocates. Their primary defense mechanism is projection. They anticipate the worst and play out apocalyptic scenes and situations in their heads. Fears trap them in their mind. In that sense, Sixes are pessimistic. They avoid doubt and are pernickety about following rules, tried and tested schemes, protocols and procedures. But in moments of crisis, they can overcome their fear more than anyone else, sometimes heroically. Sixes need to learn to break free and make decisions on their own. Unredeemed Sixes take themselves too seriously, have little humor. Sixes need to realize that, "There is no fear in love. But perfect love casts out fear" (1 John 4:18 NIV).

Sixes are ambivalent about closeness. Paradoxically, they become dependent on someone to become independent. Their suspicions can lead them into self-isolation. Healthy Sixes excel technologically; they are practical problem-solvers, teachers, social commentators, attracted to law and the sciences. Self-preservative Sixes tend to make friends slowly; they don't easily disguise their anxiety or neediness. Social Sixes handle their anxiety by looking to allies for support. Social Sixes want to fit in; they look for reassurances and are attracted to groups and causes. They are congenial. Sexual Sixes develop strength, power and physical attractiveness; they are highly aware of their sex appeal. They can become erratic in behavior and depressive, even paranoid.

Because Sixes fear they will lose their independence they invest themselves in organizations they believe will help them survive and thrive. They are impulsive and indecisive, often consulting with too many people. They frequently worry about their future, seeking assurance and insurance. Sixes hedge their bets. Sixes are constantly conscious of their fears and so are energized by them. Fear can propel them. They cope with fear by going with it or against it. They dislike many options and sudden changes. They remain vigilant, watchful, hyperalert but can get very stressed and catastrophize. They blame and complain.

Their potential pathology is paranoid or borderline personality disorder, the symptoms of which include intense anxiety, panic attacks, acute feelings of inferiority, depression, fear of losing support from others, dependency commingled with defiance, keeping 'bad company,' attachment to abusive relationships, extreme suspicion, hysterical lashing-out at perceived enemies.

Their symbolic country is masculine, authoritarian Germany. Their symbolic animal is the wolf which needs the protection of the pack, the fearful mouse, the hare in full flight and the obedient German shepherd. Probable Sixes include Sigmund Freud, J. R. R. Tolkien, Oscar Romero, Helen Palmer (of Enneagram fame), and Adolf Hitler.

Sevens

The Seven is the enthusiast, the generalist, the multitasker, the connoisseur, the energizer. Their Basic Fear is of being deprived and trapped in pain. Their Basic Desire is to be happy, to find fulfilment. Sevens radiate enthusiasm, energy and joy. They show childlike astonishment and curiosity. Sevens are playful, immediate, idealistic, cheerful, charming, optimistic, with an infectious sense of humor. They are full of plans for the future. When Sevens show up, children gather around. They paint their lives in positive colors, always protecting themselves against painful experiences. The Seven is a

Pollyanna type—everything's wonderful. The Seven is the *puer aeternus*—the eternal child, Peter Pan. Their catch cry: "I can't wait!"

The Seven is a thinking type but this is not immediately apparent. Their thinking is anticipatory. They are practical. They are widely read and highly verbal. Their minds rush from one idea to another in a fever of brainstorming and synthesizing. Sevens prefer overviews than probing one particular subject in depth. They are quick learners with agile minds. They can absorb new material quickly and have excellent body-mind coordination which makes them proficient at tennis and other sports. The Seven is the quintessential Renaissance man. Due to this, it is difficult for them to decide what to do with themselves. Their anxiety will be around the aspect of choice in their lives. They defend against this in two ways: by keeping their minds busy at all costs and by endlessly moving from one experience to another in rapid succession, searching for more sources of stimulation and satisfaction. For this reason, Sevens don't really feel that they find what they want in life. They try everything and resort to anything. They want it all. Their fast-paced thinking and living can leave them frustrated, anxious, enraged and depleted emotionally. They can end up ruining their health or their relationships.

Sevens have mastered the art of bluffing—they present themselves as knowing about everything. Their storytelling amuses; their chatter mystifies and fascinates. They often find it difficult to tie themselves down to one career or book or project. They prefer to be self-employed as they are by nature anti-authoritarian. They carry out several tasks at once.

Their basic defense mechanism is rationalization, mainly because they can find ways out of dealing with difficulties. Sevens refuse to feel pain—indeed, they avoid it at all costs. Many Sevens as children were afraid of the dark. Ireland is the land of the Sevens with the famous Irish *craic* and love of stories. Sevens are unhappy when others are unhappy. At times, Sevens know that their smiles conceal deep sadness.

If their main gift is joy, the sin of the Seven is intemperance, gluttony. Their motto: more is better. This goes for eating and drinking but also in relation to beginning even more projects, seeking more recognition, exaggerating everything, wanting more, buying more, possessing more, living in more beautiful places. Sevens are exuberant, cheerful, good-humored—they talk too much—and have an excessive need for fun and pleasure and joy. In fact, they have an uncanny flair for finding fun. There will always be something to laugh about even in the darkest times. They love fantasy. Sevens

The Enneagram: Nine Foundational Fears

are epicureans. If you criticize a Seven, they will smile and simply ignore it, dismissing it with a few witty remarks. They can also work too much, becoming workaholics. Unredeemed Sevens assume they can fashion their own happiness. Redeemed Sevens embody sober joy. The energy of the Seven is often a retreat from reality. They need to live realistically, in the beautiful and painful present, rather than harking back to the past or anticipating the future through daydreaming. They also need to overcome their psychological fear of pain. They should meditate and slow down, taking time to savor stimuli. Sevens are influenced by the separation phase of ego development from mother; they focus on transitional objects such as toys and teddy-bears, games and other distractions to assuage their anxiety.

Healthy Sevens are entertainers, creative, positive, witty; they have cooperative spirits and organizational abilities. They seem to accomplish a great deal without too much effort. They give the impression of ease. They seek variety and interact well with all sorts of people. They don't like to be alone and are torn between the grass is greener elsewhere and wanting a deeper commitment and connection with what is present. There is the possibility of substance abuse. Redeemed Sevens are materialistic in the broadest sense, are driven to material success and positions of power and prominence. They pursue their desires strategically. They have a taste for the outrageous. They dislike boundaries and limitations. Sevens frequently complain about boredom. They are lavish with money and live in the fast lane. They like to keep all options open. They overdo everything. Partially completed projects lie in their wake. Thy often 'wing' it. Sevens can become extremely demanding and intolerant especially when nothing is happening fast enough. Sevens are assertive and impatient. They leap before they look. Escapism and addiction can become a real problem for Sevens. Sevens crave. They need structure.

Self-preservative Sevens are classic consumers; they believe in pampering themselves. Less healthy Sevens get impatient when their needs are not instantly met, and cranky and thoughtless. They can become reckless and squander their resources through gambling and excessive eating and drinking and indulgence in general. Unredeemed Sevens are, in short, profligates. They are never satisfied. Their thinking is anticipating.

Sevens hate missing out on anything. Their fear is FOMO (the Fear Of Missing Out). They fear that there will not be enough of what they need. They also fear that their actions are bringing them anxiety. Hysterical activity will alternate with deep depression. They will often surround themselves with and cultivate a group of friends who will share their enthusiasms and interests. Sevens get frustrated by the slow pace of others. Sevens plan an endless succession of social gatherings and events, which are seldom brought to conclusion.

Sexual Sevens look beyond the ordinary. They have a heightened imagination. Such Sevens feel hypnotized and dazzled by a new object of desire. They fantasize about the future. Less healthy sexual Sevens can become fickle and restless. They will pursue the latest fads. Disappointment and dissatisfaction will soon follow.

Their potential pathology is manic-depressive or histrionic personality disorder with its symptoms of extreme dissipation, attempts to escape anxiety, addictions, impulsiveness and infantile reactions, compulsive activities, elated mood, out of control periods, mania, depression, mood swings and periods of panic and paralyzing terror.

Sevens are brilliant, multifaceted personalities and have their feet on the ground. They are big-picture people and maintain discipline. Their infectious enthusiasm is contagious, but they need to stay connected with presence. They are hedonistic, anti-conventional, and never grow up. Perhaps their greatest gift is to see the mystical in the mundane, the spiritual in the material.

The symbolic animal of the Seven is the monkey (monkey-mind) and the butterfly, as well as the playful otter and the skittish squirrel. The Seven is always searching for new adventures and experiences.

Probable Sevens include St. Francis of Assisi, Wolfgang Amadeus Mozart, Benjamin Franklin, and Oscar Wilde.

Eights

Eights are strong and mighty, open, honest and direct, reliable, responsible, trustworthy, forthright and energetic. They are gut types (like Eights, Nines and Ones). Eights have been called bullies. They are challengers, domineering, driven, self-confident, decisive, powerful, combative, charismatic. They are addicted to risk. Theirs is an unbridled ravenousness. Their 'sin' is lust. They don't acknowledge their fear which causes the reaction-formation of confrontation. Their Basic Fear is of being harmed or controlled by others. Their Basic Desire is to protect themselves and determine their own course in life. They are vital and willful. They are independent, individualistic and don't like being indebted to anyone. They fear being disempowered.

As children, they may have felt they were pushed around or overlooked, or they were given instructions by parents to "fight back" and "take it like a man." Some Eights develop their hardness as a counter-reaction to parents who were too liberal. Many Eights had to become adults at an early age. They tend to grow up quickly. Eights are mavericks and rebels.

Eights don't apologize for making mistakes. They construe that as weakness. Unlike Ones, Eights pull no punches. They get their energy from displaying their power. Eights are inflexible. They treat others and themselves harshly. Their aggression similarly comes from their gut. It comes especially to the fore where they see an injustice or spot something hypocritical. Eights see life as essentially hostile. They will even seek out or create conflict. They enjoy being *against*. But they do side with the weak in society. Buried deep within the Eight is a vulnerable, innocent inner child, which they sometimes discover in others and want to protect. They adopt the cause of the 'little people' and the poor. Their tough facades hide a vulnerability. They present an imposing exterior to the world mainly because they fear rejection. They build up their egos to protect themselves. They relate through anger, by "confrontational intimacy."

Eights hate unclear messages and imaginary slights to their self-esteem. They are authoritative. Eights are competitive in sports. They can spot weaknesses in others, which they will manipulate for their own advantage, remorselessly. They suffer from little guilt. Eights are not diplomats! They are leaders and revolutionaries. They avoid weakness and helplessness like the plague. They believe themselves to be absolutely correct and are intolerant of dissent, insubordination or counter arguments. They often treat colleagues or friends like doormats. They elevate themselves in hierarchies and fit people into "friend-foe" schemas. You will never win in a dispute with an Eight. They endure pain heroically, and sometimes even enjoy it. They seldom show fear. They live on the edge, especially of catastrophe. They are larger than life. Their main defense mechanism is denial. They will disavow anything that doesn't fit in with their view of things, with their concept of what's right and true, with their perspective on life. They will violate other people for pleasure or power and possess them out of passion.

Unredeemed Eights have no respect really for the dignity of the other, on whom they will place impossibly high demands. Eights are inclined towards excessive instinctual satisfaction, enjoying food, alcohol and sex without guilt. Like Sevens (albeit in different ways) they have a lust for life. They enjoy power and get furious if outfoxed or deceived. They demand obedience from everybody. Unredeemed Eights are merciless. Healthy Eights have a passion for life, are magnanimous, generous and gregarious.

Eights hate looking inside themselves. They are afraid of their soft core. They certainly aren't even aware of their tenderness, though they do notice it in others, such as children or animals. The Eight's mask of strength conceals an insecurity and feelings of inferiority. Eights have to be boss. They are very black and white. They seek clarity. They don't do nuance or subtlety. They are people of polar oppositions. "Whoever is not with me, is against me." All Eights are called to compassion. Eights pursue power, especially over others. They also seek to narcotize their feelings with alcohol and celebrations. They need to be right; they don't allow for compromise and others are expected to follow and obey. They like to humiliate and intimidate. They are industrious but lack emotional connection. Healthy Eights have a quick mind and are action oriented. They have an impact on the world. They have big plans, are outgoing and talkative. They are pragmatic but not overly concerned with pleasing others. Eights are entrepreneurial wheeler-dealers. Eights take on challenges but fear they may not have enough resources to succeed with their projects. They worry that others won't give them their due. They fear others won't back them up or will turn against them. They don't trust easily. Humor is important to them. Eights want to be respected, revered at times. Their penchant for control, can assume the form of self-mastery.

Self-preservative Eights are no-nonsense people, domestic, materialistic; they want money for power. They worry about protecting their possessions. They are very territorial. In the unhealthy range, self-preservative Eights become bullies and thieves. They see life as a jungle, where only the fittest survive. Social Eights create powerful bonds, but they can take friends for granted. They enjoy debates; the more heated the better. Unhealthy social Eights can become antisocial loners and experience feelings of rejection and betrayal. Often, they are reckless, self-destructive and prone to substance abuse. Sexual Eights are intense, humorous—they like being the bad boy. Sexually, they can play rough, but they lose interest of they win too easily in debate or conquest. They demand loyalty and attention. In the unhealthy range, sexual Eights can completely control and dominate their partner, seeing their partner as a possession or plaything, becoming acutely jealous.

The Eight needs to feel superior and self-sufficient, autonomous. They see themselves as rocks, pushing against the world. They live intensely. They assert their will over the environment, including other people. They are adrenaline junkies. They love to beat the odds. They are always looking for the 'big break' and bargaining power. They always want to be in charge. They radiate a force field around themselves. They are stimulated by conflict. Intimacy becomes a real problem for them. They express themselves through sexuality and physical prowess rather than through emotion. They expend huge amounts of energy. Eights frequently suffer from heart attacks, strokes, cancer and high blood pressure.

Eights are straight talkers. They don't beat around the bush. They discover boundaries by testing them all the time. They don't take direction. They bulldoze their way through life, intimidating others who get in their way. Periods of stress can cause them to become highly strung. At times, they become solitary figures.

Their potential pathology is antisocial personality disorder (sadistic and paranoid), symptoms of which include paranoid feelings of being betrayed, increasing social isolation and bitterness, callous hard-heartedness, lack of empathy and conscience, episodic outbursts of rage, violence and physical destructiveness, plotting vengeance and retaliation. They see themselves as the outlaw striking back at society (sociopathic).

Spain is the symbolic country of Eights—the land of *machismo*. The bull is their symbolic animal, as well as the rhinoceros, the rattlesnake, and the tiger, as all these animals are aggressive and full of phallic power.

Probable Eights include Martin Luther King (a redeemed Eight), Che Guevara, John Wayne, Ernest Hemingway, Jesse Jackson, Joseph Stalin, Karl Marx, Franklin D. Roosevelt, Mikhail GOrbachev, Bette Davis, Joan Crawford, Sean Connery, Donald Trump, and Nelson Mandela (another redeemed Eight).

Nines

Point Nine is the beginning and endpoint of the Enneagram. It represents the sum of all types. Nines are peacemakers and mediators. Nine describes the original human essence. Without civilization, we would all be Nines. Nines remind us of the spiritual nature of reality. The Nine is the healer, the optimist, the reconciler, the comforter, and nobody special. Their Basic Fear is the fear of loss and separation. Their Basic Desire is to maintain peace of mind.

Nines are receptive, reassuring, affable, complacent. They are innocent and inclusive. Nines have a vagueness about them, especially in relation to understanding themselves. They lack focus and determination.

They retreat into their minds. They are generalists, not masters of knowledge. Their default position is avoidance. They avoid taking hard decisions and put off important tasks and responsibilities. They lack courage or just don't see themselves as important enough. In childhood, many Nines were overlooked and ignored, while others were spoiled or swamped. The interest of parents or siblings took preference over their own needs and wants. They always want to understand both sides of an argument. Nines are lovable. They are charming and malleable. They are simple, uncomplicated and honest. They prefer to deny the disturbing things in life. Nines numb out. They stay in the background.

Nines belittle themselves. They seem humble. However, this conceals a false modesty and a fear of revealing themselves. They are convinced that they are not special. They seldom attract the attention of others. Nines are unassuming, self-effacing. They get caught up in nonessential activities.

Their defense mechanism is narcosis. Because they feel inadequate to life's challenges and crises, they often take refuge in some sort of addiction, be it alcohol or nicotine. They seek stimulants and sensations from outside themselves. Nines are absent-minded, befuddled and live dreamily. They withdraw when distressed. Nines really need to develop a sense of themselves and their inner worth and discover their inner drive. Their root sin is laziness. By nature, Nines are easy-going, but they lack initiative. They will not let themselves be tied down. They like their creaturely comforts, finding most things to be not worth the effort. Nines are relaxed, to say the least. Sometimes, there is no sign of life in them. Nines are passive and very slow to express their anger; when they do, it explodes out of them. Nines don't like life to be complicated—they seek and treasure simplicity. They want no fuss. They are down to earth, even-tempered, non-threatening, unflappable. They talk in a monotone manner. At least, one Enneagram writers calls Nines "slugs." They are stubborn and lack imagination and can fixate on trivialities. Nines lumber their way through life.

Unredeemed Nines can avoid everything—from themselves to the world. They have none of the defense mechanisms of the other types. They deaden inner and outer conflict. They are reposeful and can have a calming effect on others. In relationships, Nines oscillate between having a deep desire for autonomy and a wish for symbiosis and fusion with the other. Nines waver, procrastinate and put off nearly everything. They live by harmony and peace (described by St. Augustine as "the tranquillity of order").[24] They have no clear standpoints or positions. They are disarming

---

24. Augustine, *City of God*, 19.13.

and get away with things. Nines have a gentle disposition. They are skilled at sloth. Nines need to be wanted. Theirs is a secret cynicism. Nines seek wholeness and unity. They like routine and ordered structure lest they capitulate to passive fatalism. Nines are patient and don't take themselves, or anything else for that matter, too seriously.

Self-preservative Nines enjoy simple pleasures. In the unhealthy range, they become fatigued and ineffectual—and addicted. The social Nine leads a life of conformism, comfort and convention. They find it hard to say no. In the unhealthy range, they become depressed, needy, emotionally flat and insecure. The sexual Nine often gravitates to aggressive types. They seek a complete partnership. They idealize the other, then become critical and demanding. They are romantic but lack a cohesive core identity. They like to merge with their partner.

Nines are overly accommodating; they say yes to everything and so their repressed resentment emerges in passive-aggressive behavior. They fear that conflicts in the house will ruin their peace of mind and jeopardize their freedom. They avoid personal conflicts by going along with others. They worry that their fragile peace will be disrupted; they are afraid that others will demand from them, thus arousing their anxiety and unsettling them. Nines fear that they will be forced to deal with their problems. Indeed, Nines fear acknowledging reality at all, which they feel unable to face. The Nine is the boy in the bubble. Nines live life at a long and safe distance. They focus more on their relationships than themselves. Nines are detached. Unredeemed Nines check out on life and withdraw into their Inner Sanctum (conflict-free zone) where they are masters of their fate, where no people or problems can intrude. Here, they are content to fantasize their days away.

Nines snooze through life, giving the distinct impression that they are turned off. They are accommodating but don't want to be affected by anything. Nines are brick walls; their shutters are down. They can become prey to paranoid suspicions. Their potential pathology is dissociative disorders, the symptoms of which include denial of serious financial or health or personal problems, resistance and obstinacy especially in relation to getting help, repressed vitality, neglectfulness and a sense of inadequacy, dependency on others and allowing themselves to be exploited, emotional flatness and chronic depression, as well as extreme dissociation (deeply disconnected).

Their symbolic animal is the elephant who stands around all day; also, the (playful) whale and dolphin. The country of Nines is Mexico; the image of the Nine is of one wearing a sombrero and taking an afternoon siesta.

There are few prominent Nines. Gerald Ford was a Nine, as was C. G. Jung. Pope John XXIII was a redeemed Nine. Other Nines include Ronald Reagan, Kevin Costner, Whoopi Goldberg, Ingrid Bergman, Abraham Lincoln, and the Dalai Lama (another redeemed Nine).

Last Word

When all types lose Presence, personality takes over and the Self becomes eclipsed by ego. When we become liberated from our Basic Fear and Basic Desire, there is a reversal of everything that has happened in the lower levels of development. When essence emerges, identifications dissolve and so does ego, which bows out.

When Michelangelo was asked how he created a piece of sculpture, he answered that the statue already existed within the marble. Michelangelo's job was to get rid of the excess marble. Essence emerges from what is there. All types (encompassing the triple continuum of unredeemed, average, and redeemed) need to work on their foundational fears. This task of transformation is a lifelong practice.

Thus, the instinctive triad (types One, Eight, and Nine) fear that if they relax and let their guard down, they will disappear. They fear being open. If they let the world in, they fear they will disappear. They will lose their independence and freedom and be annihilated. So, these three types are called to do precisely that. The feeling triad (types Two, Three, and Four) fear that if they stop identifying with their image of themselves their worthlessness will be exposed, and they will lose the possibility of experiencing love. They fear that they are unlovable, horrible people deep down. These types have to let go of these ego agendas and personality constructs. The thinking triad of Five, Six and Seven fear that if they stop figuring things out the ground will not support them. They fear the world can't be trusted. They fear that without their mental activity they will be left vulnerable, and everything will fall to pieces, that things will collapse, and they will be lost. But they will swim, not sink. Every type must face into their fundamental fears and seek to dissolve them. This is done by the recovery and rediscovery of the true Self. Essence is the beyond of personality. But it's also right under our nose. Essence already exists in its entirety only always now.

Conclusion

Final Thoughts

WE NEED TO ATTUNE ourselves less with our ego-personalities and more with our natural essence. Of course, we need to get in to touch with our feelings too (far better, though, to engage more with the heart), but we also need to get in touch with our minds where the feelings originate. The problem is when I start *identifying* with my emotions, with one particular feeling, be it fear or anger. Why? Because emotions are not me myself. If I think my feelings are me, then I have lost my freedom. What happens when one identifies with a given emotion? Remember that emotions, *by their nature*, are always on the move. They move on; sometimes we don't. If we identify with an emotion, the feeling (of fear or anger) is held onto. It's appropriated as mine. It's not permitted to move on freely. I'm now no longer in flow. In fact, I'm fixed, stuck and soon I become unstuck by identifying with another emotion, which arises within me and to which I react.

To take an example: say the situation is that I have to give a talk and I am not prepared. A thought arises: "I don't think I can do this." Then a feeling: fear of failure. I see the fear as a constitutive component of myself. Therefore, the fear is justified. This is the heart of the identification. So, to keep it in existence I keep my mind glued to it. I entertain all sorts of possible scenarios and situations that prove how justified I am to hold on to this fear. My distinct impression is that the fear has me. And it won't let go. A chain of reactions is put in place. I suffer as a result. I then identify with the suffering, telling myself: 'I have to be afraid, and I have to suffer. In fact,

The Nine Faces of Fear

I'll never *not* be afraid, and I'll always suffer.' I then might reject this but only until another emotion seizes me. My mind gains momentum and runs amok. Within a short space of time, my mind is in mayhem—a minefield. We may describe these as **ANTS** in the mind: Automatic Negative Thoughts.

> "In the blackest of your moments, wait with no fear." –Rumi

Now, if I do not identify, what happens? I am not captured by the egoic-emotion. I'm no longer a prisoner or puppet but a person. Then the emotion will do what it naturally does—move. For emotions come and go. And I notice the emotion coming and going but I am not identified with it. Therefore, I do not have to keep an eye on it constantly. It can do what it wants since it's not me. The minute I experience my old emotional patterns beginning to emerge I can practice disidentification. For we are dominated by everything with which our Self is identified. However, we can control everything from which we dis-identify ourselves. Our bodily sensations, emotions and feelings, and mental contents all can enter the field of my observation. We must distinguish between the contents of the field of my consciousness and its center, which is the Self. The "I" is constant, unchanging, and self-conscious—all aware, as it is awareness itself. Who am I if I am not my thoughts and feelings, if I am not my intellect or body? I am pure consciousness. If the ego is an actor in the drama of life, the Self directs the show.

> "All the world's a stage, And all the men and women merely players. They have their exits and entrances, And one man in his time plays many parts, His acts being seven ages." – William Shakespeare

The seven ages are: the infant puking in the nurse's arms, then the whining schoolboy with his satchel and morning face, then a lover sighing with a woeful ballad, then a soldier quick to quarrel, followed by the justice and his fair round belly; the sixth stage slips into the slippered and spectacled pantaloon (an Italian comedy that is represented as a foolish old man wearing these particular close-fitting garments for the hips and legs); last scene of all that ends this strange and eventful history is second childishness and mere oblivion—"*sans* teeth, *sans* eyes, *sans* taste, *sans* everything."

> "Remember that you are an actor in a play determined by the author; if short, then short; if long, then long. If he wants you to act as a beggar, then act even that with excellence, just as a cripple,

a ruler, or a citizen. Because that is your objective: to act the role that is given to you well. To select the role is up to someone else."
–Epictetus

Five As

To conclude: we may chart a pattern of developmental growth, a *five*-point plan thus:

1. *Awareness*: becoming Self-observing and grounded in the present
2. *Acceptance*: being open-hearted and kind/compassionate especially in the face of conflict
3. *Appreciation*: being grateful for what is
4. *Action*: loving service to the world
5. *Adherence*: being committed to the practice of Self-enquiry and the discipline of daily meditation

We need to continue to practice distinguishing between the object of our fear and the fear itself, to realize that there is more to us than the fear, that there is something within us that is not afraid. This involves the ancient contemplative practice of watchfulness, of attentiveness, so we move from victim to witness. Meditation refines the silent witness within each of us. In *Into the Silent Land: The Practice of Contemplation*, Augustinian friar Martin Laird describes this witness, that which is *aware* of the afflictive emotion, that which is *aware* of clinging to it or fleeing from it, as itself free of the affliction, free of the clinging, free of the fleeing. A second important point to emphasize is the need to be *still* in the midst of the fear. Fear may be present, but we will not be afraid of fear. We dissolve it rather than demand that is should be gone. We will still be aware of fear, but what is aware of the fear is free of fear. If we want to make fear grow, then run from it. Better by far to meet the emotion with stillness. Without a dedicated discipline—such as meditation—this won't be possible. Allow fear to be present but let go of the commentary on the fear. If you want to know the true nature of fear, look straight into it. Fear, anger, envy—any afflictive thought or feeling—cannot withstand a direct gaze, contends Laird. But if we feed on the *story* we are telling ourselves of our fear, anger, envy, etc., affliction thrives. Affliction feeds off the noise of the endlessly circling, commenting, chattering mind. A silent mind knows no suffering or sadness. The silent Self knows that what sees the fear is free of the fear. Meditation is the way out of the great ego-centered psychodrama. The Self that sees the mind games we play is free of all such mind games and we awake to realize we are not afraid of fear.

Finally, we say we're free but free for what? The answer that arises: enjoyment. We should seek to *express* our joy and happiness *in* the show rather than *extract* happiness and joy *from* the show. Our business in all the comings and goings is to fulfil our role/function (*ergon*) in the Great Game with detachment and the unseriousness of human affairs. It's the only way. As we watch our performance. When we loosen our identifications, we are able to play our part through love and knowledge in the grand drama without being bound by fear (or anger), or any ego-type. Such is the real meaning of freedom. *Noli Timere.*

> "And all shall be well and
> All manner of things shall be well
> When the tongues of flame are in-folded
> Into the crowned knot of fire
> And the fire and the rose are one."[1]

"Philosophy's main task is to respond to the soul's cry; to make sense of and thereby free ourselves from the hold of our griefs and fears." –Epictetus

---

1. T. S. Eliot, "Little Gidding," from *Four Quartets*.

Postscript: From Fear to Freedom

"Strange, it is a huge nothing that we fear." –Seamus Heaney

THE AIM OF PHILOSOPHY is freedom, which we may define as inner independence. We desire to be free in all our worlds because being free is being my Self. The journey is from fear and, indeed, all subjective feelings into this Great Freedom. "Free" is etymologically related to "friend." In Sanskrit, *priya* meaning "dear" or "beloved," so freedom is our beloved friend. We must hold freedom dear. Emancipation is the task of our lifetime.

On Holy Saturday 2020, Pope Francis tweeted this: "Do not be afraid; do not yield to fear. This is the message of hope. It is addressed to us, today. These are the words that God repeats to us this very night."[1] The words of Psalm 91, which are chanted by monks every evening at Compline, are more prescient than ever: "You will not fear the terror by night, nor the arrow that flies by day, nor the plague that stalks in the darkness, nor the scourge that lays waste at noon" (Ps 91:5–7 TLV)

As of October 2021, the worldwide Coronavirus death toll stands at 4.5 million and rising. There have been 219 million confirmed COVID-19 cases in 210 countries and territories. On Easter Sunday morning of 2020, Pope Francis, in his *Urbi et Orbi* address, again spoke of the fear and death which surround us, urging us to have faith in the Resurrection. Such freedom knows no bodily bounds, no sickness, no fear, and no death.

1. Pope Francis (@Pontifex), Twitter, April 11, 2020, https://twitter.com/pontifex/status/1249078509248675847?lang=en.

Postscript: From Fear to Freedom

The Statue of Liberty is an emblem erected to freedom, reminding us that the flame of freedom needs to be protected. The light of liberty is precious and powerful. The Declaration of Independence labels it an inalienable right. We are told that "the truth will make you free" (John 8:32 NJB). Truth leads to freedom. Truth, which is ever the same, is our freedom. To be free is to be Self-reliant. Such freedom ushers in fulfilment, whereas our feelings bind us. Truth and freedom are really one. We desire to be free. For example, love frees us from loneliness, food frees us from hunger, sleep frees us from tiredness, medicine frees us from disease. Full freedom is permanent not partial. But we settle for shadows of freedom, such as fame or fortune, rather than for freedom's substance. Only the mind of man can be free or bound, and this is in our control to create and change and choose. When Queen Elizabeth II visited Ireland in May 2011, commenting on the history and politics between the two nations, in a speech said, "bow to the past but don't be bound by it." Being bound is servitude. The mind creates its own cages. What binds us? Past knowledge and thoughts, feelings, and preconceptions, all of which stop us from living in the eternal now.

"Man is born free; and everywhere he is in chains."
–Jean-Jacques Rousseau

"So, every bondman in his own hand bears the power
to cancel his captivity." –William Shakespeare

In this book I have emphasized the crucial importance of inner, and not just external freedom. This spiritual freedom of the mind, Viktor Frankl called 'attitude.' Advaita calls it *bhāvanā*—it is the only aspect of the being that doesn't bind. Real freedom is freedom from ignorance of our true nature (our primary purpose in life is to come to know ourselves), inequality (the disease of difference, from which preference and duality arise) and desire, which is inversely proportional to fear. The more we desire and don't attain that which we desire, the more we fear. And if attained, we fear losing that which we have obtained. Desire narrows our lives, constricts us, sets aside love. We pursue what we desire. The only desire worth having is the desire for liberation. Freedom or liberation (*liber* in Latin means "free") for what? To enjoy the creation (our secondary purpose in life) and not to take it too seriously. The nature of the creation is that it's designed on dependency; we depend on so many external things. Internal freedom, by contrast, is independence. *Three* things are needed: measure in the body with sleep and food etc; reason in the mind; and love (rather than feelings) in the heart. One's inner world is spirit. Spirit is freedom, is happiness. To put it another way, absolute freedom is spirit. It's ever available, though seldom fully availed of. It is our essential nature.

Karl Marx wanted to free the proletariat from their chains, but he saw freedom in terms of the material rather than the mental. True freedom—emancipation—is the state of not being enslaved by ego, fear, or hobgoblins of the mind. Liberation lies in acceptance of reality as it unfolds, emerges, reveals itself. Such is the real meaning of emancipation and enlightenment. *Moksha* is the Sanskrit word, derived from *muc* meaning "free." Real freedom is the transformation involved in seeing the truth beyond the veil (*maya*) of appearance and the fog of ignorance. Freedom is being present. It comes as our life in discursive thought diminishes and our experience of the present moment predominates in consciousness. Such freedom is the presence of unity, is bliss, and the ultimate aim and end of our existence. It is also living from the deep realization that the Self in its innermost nature is free, fearless, and fulfilled.

> "Freedom is the open window through which pours the sunlight of the human spirit and human dignity." –Herbert Hoover

Bibliography

Assagioli, Roberto. *Psychosynthesis: A Manual of Principles and Techniques.* New York: Hobbs, Dorman, & Co., 1965.
———. *Transpersonal Development: The Dimension Beyond Psychosynthesis.* Findhorn, UK: Smiling Wisdom, 2007.
Augustine, St. *City of God.* Translated by Henry Bettenson. New York: Penguin, 2004.
Aurelius, Marcus. *Meditations.* Translated by Gregory Hays. New York: Modern Library, 2002.
Bourgeault, Cynthia. *The Holy Trinity and the Law of Three: Discovering the Radical Truth at the Heart of Christianity.* Boston: Shambhala, 2013.
Confucius. *The Analects.* Translated by D. C. Lau. New York: Penguin, 1979.
Costello, Stephen J. *Applied Logotherapy: Viktor Frankl's Philosophical Psychology.* Newcastle upon Tyne: Cambridge Scholars, 2019.
———. *Between Speech and Silence.* Eugene, OR: Pickwick, forthcoming.
———. *Dynamics of Discernment: A Guide to Good Decision-Making.* Eugene, OR: Pickwick, forthcoming.
———. *Philosophy and the Flow of Presence: Desire, Drama, and the Divine Ground of Being.* Newcastle upon Tyne: Cambridge Scholars, 2013.
Dickens, Charles. *A Tale of Two Cities.* New York: Dover, 1998.
Dunne, Tad. *Enneatypes: Method and Spirit.* Universal, 1999.
Eckhart, Meister. *Sermons and Treatises.* London: Element, 1987.
Ellis, Albert. *Reason and Emotion.* New York: Stuart, 1962.
Emerson, Ralph Waldo. *The Essays of Ralph Waldo Emerson.* Cambridge: Belknap, 1987.
Epictetus. *The Art of Living: The Classical Manual on Virtue, Happiness, and Effectiveness.* Translated by Sharon Lebell. London: HarperOne, 2007.
———. *Discourses.* Books I–IV. Translated by P. E. Matheson. Mineola, NY: Dover, 2004.
———. *The Enchiridion.* Translated by Thomas W. Higginson. 2nd ed. New York: Liberal Arts, 1955.
———. *Handbook of Epictetus.* Translated with introduction and annotations by Nicholas White. Indianapolis: Hackett, 1983.

Bibliography

———. *How to Be Free: An Ancient Guide to the Stoic Life*. Translated by A. A. Long. Princeton: Princeton University Press, 2019.
Epicurus. *Principal Doctrines and Letter to Menoeceus*. CreateSpace, 2017.
Frankl, Viktor. *The Will to Meaning: Foundations and Applications of Logotherapy*. New York: Meridian, 1988.
Goethe, Johann Wolfgang von. *Selected Poetry*. New York: Penguin, 2005.
Goleman, Daniel. *Emotional Intelligence*. London: Bloomsbury, 1996.
Gurdjieff, G. I. *In Search of Being: The Fourth Way to Consciousness*. Boston: Shambhala, 2021.
Hadot, Pierre. *Philosophy as a Way of Life: Spiritual Exercises from Socrates to Foucault*. Edited with an introduction by Arnold I. Davidson. Translated by Michael Chase. Maiden, MA: Blackwell, 1995.
———. *The Present Alone Is Our Happiness*. Translated by Marc Djaballah. Stanford: Stanford University Press, 2009.
———. *What is Ancient Philosophy?* Translated by Michael Chase. Cambridge: Harvard University Press, 2002.
Hanh, Thich Nhat. *Fear*. London: Rider, 2012.
Harris, William B. *Restraining Rage: The Ideology of Anger Control in Classical Antiquity*. Cambridge: Harvard University Press, 2004.
Heaney, Seamus. *New Selected Poems, 1988-2013*. New York: Faber and Faber, 2014.
Horney, Karen. *Neurosis and Human Growth*. New York: Norton, 1991.
Irvine, William. *A Slap in the Face: Why Insults Hurt—And Why They Shouldn't*. Oxford: Oxford University Press, 2013.
James, William. *The Principles of Psychology*. New York: Dover, 2000.
Jeffers, Susan. *Feel the Fear and Do It Anyway*. London: Vermilion, 1987.
Jung, C. G. *Letters of C. G. Jung, Volume 2: 1951–1961*. Edited by Adler Gerhard and Aniela Jaffé. New York: Routledge, 1976.
Keller, Helen. *The Story of My Life*. New York: Penguin, 2010.
Laird, Martin. *Into the Silent Land: The Practice of Contemplation*. London: Darton, Longman, and Todd, 2006.
Lonergan, Bernard. *Insight: A Study of Human Understanding*. Edited by Frederick Crowe and Robert Doran. Collected Works of Bernard Lonergan 3. Toronto: University of Toronto Press, 1992.
Lorenz, Konrad. *On Aggression*. London: Methuen, 1963.
Lyons, Linda. "What Frightens America's Youth? Teens Have Host of Fears." *Gallup*, March 29, 2005. https://news.gallup.com/poll/15439/what-frightens-americas-youth.aspx.
Machado, Antonio. *Poesías Completas*. Madrid: Espasa-Calpe, 1984.
Maitri, Sandra. *The Spiritual Dimension of the Enneagram*. London: Penguin, 2001.
Milton, John. *Paradise Lost*. Alma, 2019.
Montaigne, Michel de. "On Fear." In *The Complete Essays*, translated and edited by M. A. Screech, 81–84. London: Penguin, 1993.
Murdoch, Iris. *The Sovereignty of Good*. London: Routledge & Kegan Paul, 1970.
Palmer, Helen. *The Enneagram: Understanding Yourself and Others in Your Life*. San Francisco: Harper & Row, 1988.
Plato. *Complete Works*. Edited with introduction and notes by John M. Cooper. Indianapolis, IN: Hackett, 1997.
Plutarch. *Moralia (Moral Essays)*. Vol. 6. Translated by W. C. Helmbold. Loeb Classical Library 337. Cambridge: Harvard University Press, 1939.

Bibliography

Plutchik, Robert. *The Emotions*. Lanham, MD: University Press of America, 1991.
Rilke, Maria Rainer. *Selected Poems*. Oxford: Oxford University Press, 2011.
Riso, Don, and Russ Hudson. *The Wisdom of the Enneagram: The Complete Guide to Ppsychological and Spiritual Growth for the Nine Personality Types*. New York: Bantam, 1999.
Rohr, Richard. *Discovering the Enneagram: An Ancient Tool for a New Spiritual Journey*. New York: Crossroad, 1999.
Rufus, Musonius. *Lectures and Sayings*. CreateSpace, 2011.
Russell, Bertrand. *The Conquest of Happiness*. London: Routledge, 2008.
Rumi. *Selected Poems*. New York: Penguin, 2021.
Saraswati, Shantanand. *Good Company: An Anthology of Sayings, Stories, and Answers to Questions*. London: Study Society, 2017.
Seneca. *Moral Essays, Volume 1*. Translated by John W. Basore. Loeb Classical Library 214. Cambridge: Harvard University Press, 1928.
Sivananda, Sri Swami. *Conquest of Fear*. 5th ed. Shivananda Nagar, India: Divine Life Society, 1997. https://www.dlshq.org/download/conquest-of-fear/.
Spinoza, Benedict de. *Ethics*. Translated by Edwin Curley. New York: Penguin, 2005.
Svendsen, Lars. *A Philosophy of Fear*. Translated by John Irons. London: Reaktion, 2008.
Tagore, Rabindranath. *Collected Poems and Plays*. New Delhi: Rupa, 2002.
Wagner, Jerome. *Nine Lenses on the World: The Enneagram Perspective*. Evanston, IL: NineLens, 2010.
Wittgenstein, Ludwig. *Philosophical Investigations*. Translated by G. E. M. Anscombe et al. Malden, MA: Wiley-Blackwell, 2009.
———. *Tractatus Logico-Philosophicus*. Translated by D. F. Pears and B. F. McGuinness. London: Routledge, 2001.